The Everyday Chef

HOLIDAY
MEALS

Celebrity Press • Nashville, Tennessee

Text copyright © 1997 by Hambleton-Hill Publishing, Inc.
Some or all of the photographic images in this book were provided by
Digital Stock, Corporation,
1-800-545-4514

All rights reserved. No part of this publication may be reproduced or transmitted
in any form or by any means, electronic or mechanical, including photocopy,
recording, or any information storage and retrieval system,
without permission in writing from the publisher.

Published by Celebrity Press
An imprint of Hambleton-Hill Publishing, Inc.
Nashville, Tennessee 37218

Printed and bound in the United States of America

ISBN 1-58029-018-3

10 9 8 7 6 5 4 3 2 1

The authors and publisher have made every effort in the preparation of this book to
ensure the accuracy of the information. However, the information in this book is
sold without warranty, either express or implied. Neither the authors nor
Hambleton-Hill Publishing, Inc. will be liable for any damages caused or
alleged to be caused directly, indirectly, incidentally, or consequentially
by the recipes or any other information in this book.

Graphic Design/Art Direction
John Laughlin

Contents

Hors d'oeuvres & Beverages 5

Entrées 13

Stuffings & Gravies 23

Vegetables & Side Dishes 29

Casseroles 37

Leftover Solutions 43

Dessert Recipes 49

Candies & Cookies 57

Index 64

Conversion Table

Metric Conversions

1/8 teaspoon = .05 ml
1/4 teaspoon = 1 ml
1/2 teaspoon = 2 ml
1 teaspoon = 5 ml
1 tablespoon = 3 teaspoons = 15 ml
1/8 cup = 1 fluid ounce = 30 ml
1/4 cup = 2 fluid ounces = 60 ml
1/3 cup = 3 fluid ounces = 90 ml
1/2 cup = 4 fluid ounces = 120 ml
2/3 cup = 5 fluid ounces = 150 ml

3/4 cup = 6 fluid ounces = 180 ml
1 cup = 8 fluid ounces = 240 ml
2 cups = 1 pint = 480 ml
2 pints = 1 liter
1 quart = 1 liter
1/2 inch = 1.25 centimeters
1 inch = 2.5 centimeters
1 ounce = 30 grams
1 pound = 0.5 kilogram

Oven Temperatures

Fahrenheit	Celsius
250°F	120°C
275°F	140°C
300°F	150°C
325°F	160°C
350°F	180°C
375°F	190°C
400°F	200°C
425°F	220°C
450°F	230°C

Baking Dish Sizes

American	Metric
8-inch round baking dish	20-centimeter dish
9-inch round baking dish	23-centimeter dish
11 x 7 x 2-inch baking dish	28 x 18 x 4-centimeter dish
12 x 8 x 2-inch baking dish	30 x 19 x 5-centimeter dish
9 x 5 x 3-inch baking dish	23 x 13 x 6-centimeter dish
1 1/2-quart casserole	1.5-liter casserole
2-quart casserole	2-liter casserole

Hors d'oeuvres & Beverages

Batter:
A thin mixture of flour and liquid that is combined with other ingredients to make foods such as cakes.

Beat:
To mix ingredients until smooth by using a quick stirring motion or an electric mixer.

Barbecued Chicken Wings

3/4 c. olive oil
1/2 c. onion, chopped
1 1/4 c. water
1/2 c. wine vinegar
4 tbsp. Worcestershire sauce
1/2 c. lemon juice
5 tbsp. brown sugar
1 tbsp. paprika
2 1/2 c. catsup
salt and pepper to taste
4 lb. chicken wings

Heat the olive oil in a large skillet. Add the onion and sauté until translucent. Add all remaining ingredients except the chicken wings. Simmer over medium-low heat for 20–25 minutes. Remove from heat and allow to cool thoroughly.

Place the chicken wings in a bowl with a tight-fitting lid. Cover with sauce, replace the lid, and toss to coat. Marinate in the refrigerator for 1–2 days. Grill for 20 minutes, or until done, basting often.

Spicy Crab Dip

8 oz. crab meat, shredded
8 oz. cream cheese, softened
1 onion, minced
1 clove garlic, minced
1 tsp. hot sauce
3 tbsp. Parmesan cheese, grated

Mix the crab meat, cream cheese, onion, garlic, and hot sauce. Pour into a casserole dish and top with Parmesan cheese. Bake at 350°F until it bubbles and browns. Serve warm with toasted bread or crackers.

Spinach Dip

1 1/2 c. mayonnaise
1 c. sour cream
1 box Knorr's leek soup mix
1/4 tsp. salt
2 boxes frozen chopped spinach, thawed
1 small can water chestnuts, chopped
2 green onions, chopped
2 sourdough bread rounds

In a bowl, mix the mayonnaise, sour cream, soup mix, and salt. Add the spinach and mix thoroughly. Stir in the water chestnuts and green onions.

Cut one sourdough round into a bowl and fill it with the spinach mixture. Slice the other sourdough round into bite-size pieces and toast if desired. Serve.

Shrimp Dip

1 pkg. (8 oz.) cream cheese, softened
6 oz. shrimp
3 thin slices of onion, finely diced
1 tsp. lemon juice
4 tbsp. milk

In a small mixing bowl, combine all the ingredients. Using an electric mixer set on medium speed, blend the ingredients, mashing the shrimp.

Scrape the sides of the bowl several times while mixing. Pour into a serving dish. Serve with crackers or sourdough toast.

Chili con Queso

1 1/2 tbsp. olive oil
1 1/2 tbsp. butter
1 medium onion, finely chopped
4 medium tomatoes, chopped
4 jalapeño peppers, chopped and seeded
2 pkgs. cream cheese (8 oz. each)
1 pt. half-and-half

In a large sauté pan, combine the olive oil and butter. Add the onion and sauté until translucent. Add the tomatoes and peppers. Bring the mixture to a boil and simmer for at least 15 minutes.

Using a whisk, stir in the cream cheese. When the cream cheese is melted, add the half-and-half, mixing well. Pour into a serving dish. Serve with tortilla chips or vegetable sticks.

Chicken Squares

3 oz. cream cheese
3 tbsp. butter, melted, divided
2 c. chicken, cooked, cubed
1/4 tsp. salt
1/8 tsp. pepper
2 tbsp. milk
1 tbsp. onion, minced
1 tbsp. pimento
1 pkg. (8 oz.) crescent roll dough

Preheat oven to 375°F. Blend the cream cheese and 2 tablespoons melted butter until smooth. Add the chicken, salt, pepper, milk, onion, and pimento. Stir and set aside. Divide the crescent rolls into rectangles and seal the seams. Place 1/2 cup of filling on each rectangle. Gather the four corners together and twist to seal. Pinch the edges together to seal them. Brush with remaining melted butter. Bake on an ungreased cookie sheet for 20–25 minutes.

Orange Wassail

2 qt. orange juice
2 qt. apple juice
1 qt. cranberry juice cocktail
1 can (12 oz.) frozen lemonade concentrate, thawed and undiluted
1 (2-inch) stick cinnamon
1 tbsp. whole cloves
2 oranges, sliced

Combine orange juice, apple juice, cranberry juice, lemonade concentrate, and cinnamon stick in a large saucepan.

Insert the cloves into the orange slices and drop them into the juice mixture.

Cook over medium-high heat until thoroughly heated. Serve hot.

Roasted Garlic and Broccoli Cheese Spread

2 tbsp. roasted garlic
1/2 lb. broccoli, minced
8 oz. cream cheese
2 tsp. chives

Squeeze soft garlic from roasted cloves and set aside. Steam broccoli for 5 minutes. Allow to cool.

Combine broccoli, garlic, cream cheese and chives in a food processor. Process until mixture is smooth. Chill for 3 hours before serving with fresh vegetables for dipping.

Potstickers

Dough:
2 c. all-purpose flour
1/2 c. water

Filling:
1/2 lb. ground pork
1/2 small Chinese cabbage, cored and chopped
1 green onion, coarsely chopped
2 slices fresh ginger, minced
2 water chestnuts, chopped
1 tsp. salt
1/2 tsp. sugar
1/8 tsp. white pepper
1 tsp. sesame oil

Sauce:
5 tbsp. vegetable oil, divided
1 c. water
hot chili oil
red rice vinegar
soy sauce

In a bowl, mix the flour and 1/2 cup water together to form a ball. Turn out on a lightly floured surface and knead for 3 minutes.

Shape into a ball, cover with a damp towel, and let stand for 10 minutes.

Combine all the filling ingredients, mixing well. Refrigerate until ready to use.

Knead the dough for an additional 3 minutes. Shape it into a 1-inch wide roll. Cut off the ends. Cut the roll into 3/4-inch thick slices (you should get about 24 slices).

Press each dough slice between your palms to flatten. Using a rolling pin, roll out each slice to form a 2 1/2 to 3-inch circle. (These will be very thin.)

Leave the center of each circle slightly thicker than the edges, so that the dough will cook better.

Place 1 tablespoon of filling into the center of each circle. Fold the dough over to make a half circle and pinch the edges together firmly.

Heat a large cast iron or other heavy-bottomed skillet over moderate heat.

Add 3 tablespoons oil, swirling to coat the bottom. When oil is hot, place the potstickers, seam side up, in the skillet and shake for 30 seconds.

Pour in 1 cup water, cover, and gently boil over moderate heat for 7–8 minutes.

When the oil and water begin to sizzle, add the remaining 2 tablespoons of oil. Tilt the skillet to distribute the oil evenly. Continue to cook, uncovered. Watch carefully to prevent sticking.

When the bottoms are brown, remove the skillet from heat and carefully remove the potstickers with a spatula.

To serve, arrange the potstickers on a serving platter with the dark sides up. Combine the chili oil, vinegar, and soy sauce in equal proportions to taste and serve on the side for dipping.

Apple-Stuffed Mushrooms

32 large fresh mushrooms
vegetable cooking spray
3 tbsp. celery, finely chopped
1/2 c. apple, minced
2 tbsp. fine, dry bread crumbs
1 tbsp. parsley, chopped
2 tbsp. toasted walnuts, finely chopped
1 tbsp. blue cheese, crumbled
2 tsp. lemon juice

Preheat oven to 350°F.

Clean the mushrooms, removing the stems. Set the mushroom caps aside. Finely chop 1/3 cup of stems.

Coat a small skillet with cooking spray, and place over medium-high heat until hot. Add the chopped mushroom stems and celery. Sauté 2 minutes, or until tender. Pour into a small bowl. Stir in the apple, bread crumbs, parsley, walnuts, cheese, and lemon juice; mix well.

Spoon 1 1/2 teaspoons of mixture into each reserved mushroom cap. Place the mushrooms in a 15 x 10-inch jelly roll pan. Bake for 15 minutes.

Bacon-Wrapped Scallops

24 large sea scallops (about 2 lb.)
12 slices bacon
seasoned pepper

Preheat broiler.

Rinse scallops under cold running water; pat dry with paper towels. Cut each bacon slice crosswise in half. Wrap each scallop with a piece of bacon, securing with a toothpick. Sprinkle lightly with seasoned pepper.

Place scallops on a rack in a broiling pan so that the bacon faces the heating element. Broil 8–10 minutes, or until scallops turn opaque throughout. Using tongs, turn the scallops frequently so that the bacon browns evenly on all sides.

Christmas Punch

1 can (6 oz.) orange juice concentrate
1 can (6 oz.) lemonade concentrate
2 cans (12 oz.) pineapple juice
2 bananas
2 1/2 c. water
2 qt. lemon-lime soda
1/2 bag fresh cranberries

Blend all ingredients except the soda and cranberries. Pour into half-gallon milk cartons and freeze. Before serving, thaw to a slush. Pour into a large punch bowl. Just before serving, stir in the soda. Float fresh cranberries on top.

Holiday Eggnog

12 eggs, separated
1 c. sugar
1 qt. milk
1 c. bourbon
1/2 c. cognac
1 qt. heavy cream
grated nutmeg

Beat the egg yolks and sugar together until the mixture is thick and creamy. Add the milk, bourbon, and cognac, stirring until well mixed. When ready to serve, whip the cream into soft peaks. In a separate bowl, beat the egg whites until soft peaks form. Gently fold the whipped cream and egg whites into the liquid mixture. Pour into a large punch bowl and sprinkle with nutmeg.

Holiday Pine Cones

1 1/4 c. whole almonds
8 oz. cream cheese, softened
1/2 c. mayonnaise
5 slices bacon, cooked, crumbled
1 tbsp. green onion, chopped
1/2 tsp. dill weed
1/8 tsp. pepper

Spread almonds in a single layer in a shallow pan. Bake at 300°F for 15 minutes, stirring often, until almonds just begin to turn color. Combine cream cheese and mayonnaise; mix well. Add bacon, onion, dill and pepper; mix well. Cover and chill overnight. To serve, form cheese mixture into shapes of 2 pine cones on serving platter. Beginning at narrow end, press almonds at slight angle into cheese mixture in rows. Continue overlapping rows until all cheese is covered. Garnish with artificial pine sprigs. Serve with crackers.

Christmas Avocado Balls

6 avocados
romaine lettuce leaves
3 tsp. salt
1 1/2 tsp. white pepper
1 1/2 tsp. dried oregano
1 clove garlic, minced
2 c. olive oil
3 tbsp. red wine
3 tbsp. vinegar
paprika

Cut avocados in half and discard the pit. Scoop out avocado meat shaping into balls. A small ice cream scoop works very well. Place balls on six plates lined with lettuce leaves. In a small bowl, whisk together the rest of the ingredients, pour over avocados. Sprinkle with paprika. Serve.

A Bloomin' Onion

1 onion, well-rounded
boiling water, enough to immerse onion
ice water, enough to immerse onion
2 tbsp. flour
1 c. cracker crumbs
4 eggs, beaten

Select a well-rounded onion. Peel outer skin off. Using a small, sharp knife, divide onion into four sections by making 2 cuts crosswise, beginning at the top and cutting toward the root end, stopping about 1/2 inch from bottom. Do not cut onion apart.

Cut each section into thirds. Place onion in bowl of enough boiling water to cover it and leave for 5 minutes. The sections, or petals, will begin to open.

Remove onion from water and immerse into ice water, which will further the opening. Drain well by turning upside down on paper towel.

Put flour into paper bag, add onion and shake gently to coat, making sure it is completely covered. Roll floured onion in beaten egg, making sure it is completely covered.

Put cracker crumbs in bag, add onion, and shake gently to coat.

Refrigerate 1 hour before deep frying in oil to golden brown, 3 to 5 minutes. Cooked onion can be kept for a time in warm oven.

Serve alone or with dipping sauce.

Chicken Liver Spread

2/3 c. half-and-half
2 tbsp. butter
1 onion, minced
1 clove garlic, minced
1 lb. chicken livers
2 eggs
1/4 c. flour
2 tbsp. brandy
1 tsp. salt
1/2 tsp. sage
1/2 tsp. thyme
1/8 tsp. hot pepper sauce
chopped fresh parsley

Grease well and lightly flour five 6-oz. metal juice cans; set aside. In food processor, blend half-and-half, butter, onion and garlic.

Add livers, eggs, flour, brandy, salt, sage, thyme and pepper sauce. Process until smooth and well blended. Pour mixture into cans to within 1 inch of top. Place cans in a large bundt pan and add 2 inches hot water to pan. Place on bottom rack in preheated 350°F oven.

Bake 1 hour or until pick inserted in center comes out clean. Remove cans to rack to cool 30 minutes. With can opener, cut around bottoms of cans and push bottoms through to unmold spreads.

Chill completely. Roll in chopped parsley, wrap in plastic and again in foil. Can be refrigerated up to 1 week or frozen 3 weeks.

Cheese Log

1/2 lb. sharp cheddar cheese
1/2 lb. pimento cheese
1/2 lb. cream cheese
2 garlic cloves, minced
2 tsp. Worcestershire sauce
1/4 tsp. red pepper
2 tbsp. mayonnaise
1/4 tsp. salt
paprika (optional)
nuts, chopped (optional)

Finely grate all cheeses and mix together. Add minced garlic, Worchestershire sauce, red pepper, mayonnaise and salt. Chill for 30 minutes and then divide into thirds. Roll each in paprika or chopped nuts. Keep refrigerated until 30 minutes before serving.

Cheese Fondue

1 clove garlic, peeled, halved
1 lb. Swiss cheese, shredded
1/4 c. flour
1/4 tsp. salt
1/4 tsp. ground nutmeg
1 1/2 c. dry white wine
French bread, cut in cubes

Rub the insides and bottom of a microwave-safe fondue pot or casserole dish with garlic. Discard garlic. Combine cheese, flour, salt, and nutmeg in the prepared dish. Add wine and mix well. Heat, covered, in microwave, 6 minutes, stirring every two minutes. If cheese is not completely melted, heat an additional 30 to 60 seconds. Serve in fondue pot with bread cubes.

Spicy Cheese Ball

1/2 lb. cheddar cheese, grated
1 tsp. Worchestershire sauce
4 oz. cream cheese
1/2 tsp. hot sauce
2 tsp. onion, grated
3 tbsp. nuts, chopped, divided
2 tsp. chili sauce

Soften cheeses to room temperature. Blend all ingredients, except 2 tablespoons of nuts, in a mixer or food processor. Line small bowl with plastic wrap and spoon mixed ingredients in bowl. Completely cover ball with plastic wrap and refrigerate overnight. When ready to use, unmold, remove wrap, and roll in reserved nuts. Serve with assorted crackers.

Crackin' Jack

6 qt. popcorn, popped, unseasoned
1 c. unsalted peanuts
3 c. brown sugar
3/4 c. light corn syrup
3 sticks butter
1 1/2 tsp. salt
1/2 tsp. cream of tartar
1 1/2 tsp. baking soda

Preheat oven to 200°F. Divide the popcorn and peanuts among 2 large bowls. Oil 2 lipped cookie sheets very well and set aside. In a deep saucepan, combine the brown sugar, corn syrup, butter, salt, and cream of tartar. Insert candy thermometer.

Bring to a boil over medium heat for about 5 minutes, stirring occasionally, until the thermometer registers 260°F.

Remove from heat and quickly stir in the baking soda. Mixture will foam. Pour the syrup mixture over the popcorn and peanuts, half into each bowl. Work quickly to coat with the caramel. Spread mixture evenly on the cookie sheets and bake for 1 hour, stirring 3 times. Remove from the oven and spread on waxed paper to cool, breaking up the larger pieces. Store in airtight container.

Hot Crab Bites

1 1/2 c. crab meat, drained
1 tbsp. lemon juice
1/2 tsp. lemon peel, grated
1 green onion, minced
2 tbsp. parsley, minced
1 tsp. Worcestershire sauce
1 tsp. hot mustard
1/2 tsp. hot pepper sauce
2 tbsp. unsalted butter, melted
16 Melba toast rounds
1/2 c. sharp cheddar cheese, grated

Preheat broiler. Combine crab, lemon juice, lemon peel, green onion, parsley, Worcestershire sauce, mustard and hot pepper sauce. Taste and adjust seasonings. Brush melted butter on toast rounds and arrange in a single layer in a broiler pan. Top each round with a portion of the crab mixture, then with 1 1/2 teaspoons of cheese. Broil until cheese is melted and crab mixture is hot. Makes 16 appetizers.

Note: You may substitute deviled ham or shrimp in this recipe or use lime juice and peel instead of lemon if preferred.

Entrées

Blend:
To thoroughly mix two or more ingredients.

Boil:
To raise the temperature of a liquid until it bubbles; The boiling temperature of water is 212°F (or 100°C).

Roast Duck with Orange Sauce

1 medium whole duck
salt and pepper to taste
1 tbsp. rosemary
1 tsp. olive oil
1 apple, diced
1 orange, diced
1 onion, diced
2 c. water
3 tbsp. Grand Marnier

Preheat oven to 275°F.

Season the duck inside and out with salt, pepper, and rosemary. Glaze with olive oil.

Combine the apple, orange, and onion. Stuff duck with the mixture.

Bake for 3 1/2 hours, turning every 30 minutes and basting with juices from the pan. Remove from oven and allow to cool. Remove the stuffing and gently debone the duck.

Place the bones and stuffing in a medium pot with 2 cups water. Boil for 45 minutes; strain. Adjust the seasoning to taste. Add the Grand Marnier. Serve duck with sauce, wild rice, and vegetables.

Seasoned Ham

8 lb. smoked ham, shank half
2 tbsp. whole cloves
3/4 c. plus 2 tbsp. port wine
1 c. brown sugar, firmly packed
3 tbsp. Dijon mustard

Preheat oven to 350°F.

Score ham in a diamond pattern and stud with cloves. Place on a rack in a large roasting pan. Pour 3/4 cup port over the ham. Bake, basting occasionally with juices from pan, for 2–3 hours, or until meat reaches 140°F on a meat thermometer.

In a small bowl, combine the sugar, mustard, and 2 tablespoons port; set aside. Remove ham from oven. Increase oven temperature to 425°F. Brush sugar glaze over ham. Return to the oven and bake an additional 15 minutes, or until browned. Let stand 20 minutes before carving.

Holiday Beef Rib Eye Roast

2 cloves garlic, crushed
1 tsp. salt
1 tsp. cracked black pepper
1 tsp. dried thyme leaves
4 lb. beef rib eye roast

Currant Sauce:
1 1/2 tsp. dry mustard
1 tsp. water
12-oz. jar brown beef gravy
1/4 c. currant jelly

Heat oven to 350°F. Combine garlic, salt, pepper, and thyme; press evenly into surface of roast. Place roast on rack in shallow roasting pan. Insert meat thermometer so bulb is centered in thickest part. Do not add water or cover. Roast 18 to 22 minutes per pound for rare to medium. Remove roast from oven when meat thermometer registers 135°F for rare, 155°F for medium. Let stand 15 minutes before carving. In a small saucepan, combine sauce ingredients. Cook over medium heat 5 minutes or until bubbly, stirring occasionally. Carve roast into slices; serve with sauce.

Grilled Turkey

1 (15–20 lb.) turkey
salt and pepper
vegetable oil
2 onions, coarsely chopped
2 stalks celery, cut into 2-inch pieces
2 limes, quartered
1 lemon, quartered
1 orange, quartered
1 apple, quartered
1 qt. water
1 1/2 sticks butter
1 lemon, thinly sliced

Preheat grill to medium heat with most of the coals placed on the end opposite where turkey will be setting.

Wash and rinse the turkey, removing giblets. Pat dry with paper towels. Season the inside of turkey with salt and pepper. Rub the outside with oil. Combine the onion, celery, limes, lemon quarters, orange, and apple. Stuff turkey with the mixture, completely filling the cavities.

Melt the butter in a roasting pan. Add the water and sliced lemon, adding more lemon juice if desired. Cover turkey tightly with aluminum foil, crimping the edges. Grill for 4–6 hours, removing foil and adding smoker chips for the last hour or so.

Pork Chops with Stuffing

4 pork chops
3 bread slices, cut into cubes
2 tbsp. onion, chopped
1/4 c. butter, melted
1/3 c. plus 2 tbsp. water
1/4 tsp. poultry seasoning
1 tbsp. oil
1 can cream of mushroom soup

Preheat oven to 350°F.

Brown the pork chops, then place them in a shallow baking dish. Lightly mix together the bread, onion, butter, 2 tablespoons water, and poultry seasoning to form the stuffing. Place a mound of stuffing on top of each chop. Blend the soup and 1/3 cup water. Pour over the chops. Bake, uncovered, for 1 hour.

Pear and Maple Pork Chops

1 large ripe pear, cored and sliced
1/4 c. onion, finely chopped
1/3 c. maple syrup
1 tbsp. butter, melted
1/4 tsp. ginger
4 boneless pork loin chops
1/2 tsp. salt
1/4 tsp. pepper

In a medium bowl, combine the pear, onion, syrup, butter, and ginger. Mix well, and set aside.

Sprinkle both sides of the pork chops with salt and pepper. Spray a heavy skillet with non-stick cooking spray. Heat over medium-high heat until hot. Add the pork chops and cook for 2–3 minutes on each side, or until browned. Pour the pear mixture over the pork chops.

Reduce heat to medium-low. Cover and cook for 12–15 minutes, or until pork chops are no longer pink. Place the pork chops on a serving platter; cover to keep warm. Continue cooking the sauce over medium-high heat for 3–4 minutes, stirring constantly, until sauce is thickened. Spoon sauce over pork chops before serving.

Apple Pork Tenderloin

3 lb. pork tenderloin
2 c. onion, chopped
8 garlic cloves, peeled
2 Granny Smith apples, chopped
3/4 c. chicken broth
2 tbsp. wine vinegar
3 tbsp. olive oil
1 tbsp. honey
salt and pepper to taste

In a skillet, brown the meat on all sides. Remove the meat and place it in a roasting pan. In the same skillet used to brown the meat, sauté the onions and garlic for 5 minutes. Add the apples, and continue to sauté 2 minutes longer. Add the broth, vinegar, oil, and honey, stirring until mixed. Add salt and pepper to taste.

Pour the gravy over the pork, cover with foil, and bake for 1 to 1 1/2 hours at 325°F. Remove pork from the pan and let it stand for 10 minutes before carving. Slightly mash the gravy, and serve.

Apple Juice Roast

2 onions, sliced
2 tbsp. butter, divided
4 lb. boneless beef chuck roast
1 c. apple juice
1 tbsp. catsup
1 tsp. salt
1/4 tsp. pepper
1/4 tsp. thyme
1/4 tsp. prepared mustard
1/8 tsp. basil
3 large sweet potatoes, cut into chunks
1 tsp. lemon juice
parsley and apple rings for garnish

Cook the onions in 1 tablespoon butter in a Dutch oven until tender-crisp; set aside.

Brown the roast in the remaining butter in the Dutch oven over medium heat for 15–20 minutes, or until browned on all sides. Pierce the entire surface of the meat with a fork.

Combine the apple juice, catsup, salt, pepper, thyme, mustard, and basil. Pour mixture over the meat. Top meat with the reserved cooked onions. Cover and cook slowly for 2 1/2 hours, or until almost tender.

Brush the sweet potatoes with lemon juice to give them a bright color; add to the meat. Continue cooking, covered, for 30–40 minutes, or until meat and potatoes are tender.

Place meat and potatoes on a warm serving platter, reserving the cooking liquid. Garnish with apple rings and parsley, if desired. Serve in slices with Beef Gravy.

Beef Gravy:
reserved cooking liquid
1/2 c. water
2 tbsp. flour
salt and pepper to taste

Skim the excess fat from the cooking liquid. Add water, if needed, to make 1 1/2 cups.

In a separate bowl, mix together 1/2 cup water and 2 tablespoons flour. Gradually stir the flour mixture into the cooking liquid. Heat to boiling. Cook, stirring continuously, for 3–5 minutes. Season with salt and pepper, if desired.

Leg of Lamb with Apricot Mustard Glaze

1/4 c. apricot jam
2 tbsp. honey mustard
2 garlic cloves, chopped
2 tbsp. soy sauce
2 tbsp. olive oil
1 tsp. dried rosemary
3 lb. leg of lamb, butterflied
salt and pepper to taste
1/2 c. red wine
1 c. beef broth

Combine jam, mustard, garlic, soy sauce, olive oil, and rosemary to form a marinade. Reserve 2 tablespoons of the marinade for the serving sauce.

Brush remaining marinade over the entire surface of the leg of lamb. Season well with salt and pepper. Marinate for 30 minutes.

Broil lamb for 3 minutes on each side. Bake at 425°F, fat side up, for 20–30 minutes.

Remove from oven and let rest on a serving dish for 10 minutes.

Pour off any fat from the baking pan.

For the serving sauce, add red wine to the pan and reduce to 1 tablespoon.

Add beef broth, reserved marinade, and any extra lamb juices from the serving dish.

Bring to a boil and boil for 2 minutes. Slice the lamb in thin slices against the grain. Serve slices topped with sauce.

Basil-Stuffed Lamb Roast

3/4 c. onion, chopped
1/3 c. celery, chopped
2 cloves garlic, minced
1/4 c. olive oil
2 eggs, beaten
10 oz. frozen spinach, thawed, chopped
1/4 c. snipped parsley
3 tbsp. fresh snipped basil
1/4 tsp. dried marjoram, crushed
1/4 tsp. pepper
6 c. plain croutons
1/4 c. Parmesan cheese, grated
1/2 c. water
1 (5–7 lb.) leg of lamb, deboned and butterflied
1 tsp. dried rosemary, crushed
sprigs of fresh mint and fresh marjoram for garnish

To prepare the stuffing, cook the onion, celery, and garlic in hot olive oil until tender but not brown.

In a medium mixing bowl, stir together the eggs, spinach, parsley, basil, marjoram, and pepper. Add the onion mixture. Stir in the croutons and cheese. Drizzle with water to moisten, tossing lightly. Set aside. If necessary, remove the fell (pinkish-red, paper-thin layer) from the surface of meat. Pound meat to an even thickness. Sprinkle with rosemary. Spread the stuffing over the roast. Roll up the meat and tie it securely.

Preheat oven to 325°F. Place the roast, seam side down, on a rack in a shallow roasting pan. Insert a meat thermometer in the thickest portion of the meat. Roast, uncovered, for 1 1/2 to 2 hours, or until the meat thermometer reads 150°F.

Remove from the oven and let the roast stand for 15 minutes. Remove ties and carve.

Apple Cider Turkey

1 (12–14 lb.) turkey, giblets reserved
stuffing
1 tbsp. butter, melted
1 1/4 tsp. salt, divided
3/4 tsp. pepper, divided
4 c. water
2 c. apple cider
1/3 c. all-purpose flour
3/4 tsp. dried sage

Preheat oven to 325°F.

Fill the turkey cavity with stuffing. Truss and insert the meat thermometer. Brush butter over the breast. Sprinkle with 1/2 teaspoon salt and 1/4 teaspoon pepper. Place the turkey on a rack in a roasting pan. Roast until the juices run clear when the thigh is pierced with a fork and the meat thermometer reads 170°F, about 3 hours. Remove from pan and cover loosely with foil.

To make the gravy, place the giblets and 4 cups water in a saucepan. Bring to a boil over medium heat. Reduce heat to low and simmer 1 hour. Strain the broth and discard the giblets. Skim the fat from roasting pan juices, reserving 1/4 cup fat. Add cider to the pan. Bring to a boil over medium-high heat, scraping up browned bits. Reduce heat and simmer 5 minutes, or until reduced by half.

In saucepan, over low heat, combine the flour and reserved fat. Cook 3 minutes, stirring constantly. Stir in the cider mixture and then the giblet broth. Increase heat and simmer until thickened, about 10 minutes. Stir in the sage and remaining salt and pepper.

Salmon In Red Wine With Apricots

1 1/4 lb. salmon fillets
1/4 c. all-purpose flour
2 tbsp. vegetable oil
1 c. dry red wine
1/2 c. fish stock
1 c. dried apricots
salt to taste
pepper to taste
2 tbsp. unsalted butter

Preheat oven to 375°F. Pat the salmon dry and dust with flour, shaking off the excess. Heat the oil in a 12-inch oven-proof skillet or roasting pan over medium heat.

Add the salmon and brown on all sides. Remove to a plate and discard oil. Add the wine and stock to the skillet and bring to a boil. Replace salmon in the skillet; add the apricots and sprinkle with salt and pepper. Place, uncovered, in the oven. Cook 7 minutes.

When done, transfer skillet to the stove top and remove the fish to a carving board. Cook the liquid in the roasting pan over high heat, stirring, until it thickens slightly. Remove from heat and whisk in the butter.

Cut the salmon into 1/2-inch slices, arrange on a serving platter and spoon sauce over dish.

Autumn Fruited Chicken

12 pieces chicken
1/2 c. flour
1/4 tsp. salt
1/8 tsp. pepper
1 c. vegetable oil
1/4 stick butter
1 tbsp. brandy
1 onion, minced
3 cloves garlic, minced
2 c. mushrooms, sliced
1 1/2 c. apple wine
2 fresh pears, peeled and quartered
2 fresh apples, peeled and quartered
2 tsp. cornstarch
1/4 c. chicken stock

Shake chicken pieces in a plastic bag with flour, salt, and pepper until lightly dusted. Brown in oil with melted butter. Pour the brandy over and flame. Set aside.

Sauté the onion and garlic, adding a little more butter to the pan if needed. Place chicken, onion mixture, mushrooms, and wine in a baking dish. Add pears and apples.

Bake, covered, at 350°F for 30 minutes or until chicken is done. Remove chicken and fruit to a heated platter and thicken sauce with cornstarch mixed with a little water or chicken stock.

Serve over noodles or rice.

Holiday Turkey Fillets

1 1/2 lb. boneless turkey fillets
salt
pepper
1/2 c. golden raisins
1/2 c. dry white wine
2 tsp. capers
1 c. chicken broth, cooled
2 tsp. cornstarch
1/2 c. pine nuts, toasted

Pat the turkey fillets dry with paper towels. Sprinkle with salt and pepper.

Heat a large, non-stick skillet over medium high heat. Spray one side of the turkey fillets with non-stick vegetable oil spray.

Cook 1-2 minutes or until golden. Spray the remaining side, turn and cook for an additional minute.

Hold seared turkey fillets on a warm plate and repeat with remainder.

Add the raisins, wine, capers, and chicken broth mixed with cornstarch to the same pan, stirring constantly until slightly thickened.

Return turkey to the pan to heat. Serve turkey on individual plates with sauce spooned over the top. Sprinkle each portion with toasted pine nuts.

Baked Cornish Hens

4 Cornish game hens
1/2 c. butter
1 tsp. rosemary
2 cloves garlic, pressed
2 tbsp. lemon juice

Rub hens with butter. Combine other ingredients and use to baste hens. Bake at 350°F for 1 hour, basting with lemon mixture every 10 minutes. If serving with rice, spoon remaining lemon mixture over rice.

Baked Pineapple Chicken

20 oz. pineapple chunks
1 garlic clove, crushed
2 tsp. cornstarch
2 tsp. Worcestershire sauce
2 tsp. Dijon mustard
1 tsp. rosemary, crushed
6 half chicken breasts, deboned
1 lemon, thinly sliced

Drain pineapple, reserve juice. Combine reserved juice with garlic, cornstarch, Worcestershire sauce, mustard, and rosemary.

Arrange chicken in shallow baking pan or broiler-proof dish, skin side up.

Broil until browned. Stir sauce; pour over chicken. Bake at 400°F 30 minutes. Arrange lemon and pineapple slices around chicken. Spoon sauce from baking pan over all; continue baking 5 minutes. Garnish with fresh rosemary or parsley, if desired.

Braised Breast Of Duck With Peaches

1 tbsp. light vegetable oil
2 tbsp. butter, divided
3 firm mushrooms
2 duck livers
4 half breasts of duck, deboned
1/2 tsp. garlic, minced
2 tbsp. orange rind, grated
1 tsp. tomato paste
1 tsp. meat flavoring
1 c. chicken stock
1/4 c. orange juice
1 tbsp. honey
3/4 c. fresh peaches, pureed
1 tsp. red currant jelly
1/3 c. heavy cream, whipped
4 fresh peaches, quartered

In deep, heavy pot, heat oil. Add 1 tablespoon butter. Allow it to melt and then add mushrooms. Stir over high heat 2 minutes. Remove mushrooms and set aside. Brown livers. Remove and set aside. Lightly brown duck breasts on both sides and remove from pan. Reduce heat to low and add remaining tablespoon of butter. Add garlic and orange rind. Stir over low heat 2 minutes. Add tomato paste and meat flavoring. Blend. Add chicken stock, orange juice and honey. Stir over moderate heat until mixture boils. Add peach puree and jelly. Bring to a boil.

Place breasts in pot and coat with sauce. Cook over low heat about 20 minutes, or until done. Arrange breasts on heat-proof serving platter. Whisk whipped cream into sauce. Add mushrooms and peaches. Spoon sauce mixture over breasts. Brown top lightly under broiler. Slice livers neatly and arrange as garnish on top of dish.

Chicken & Dumplings

4 chicken breast halves
6 1/2 c. water, divided
1 1/2 c. mushrooms, sliced
3/4 c. carrots, diced
2 tbsp. onion, minced
3/4 tsp. poultry seasoning
1/2 tsp. salt
1/2 tsp. pepper
1 tsp. lemon juice
1/8 tsp. hot sauce
1 clove garlic, minced
1 1/4 c. plus 2 tbsp. flour, divided
1 tsp. baking powder
1/2 c. skim milk

Place chicken in 6 cups water with mushrooms, carrots, and onion in a large Dutch oven.

Bring to a boil. Cover. Reduce heat and simmer 45 minutes.

Remove chicken from broth and let cool separately. Discard bones and skin. Cut chicken into chunks and add to vegetable mixture. Cover and chill 8 hours.

Skim fat from broth and discard. Stir in poultry seasoning, salt, pepper, lemon juice, hot sauce and garlic. Combine 1/4 cup plus 2 tablespoons flour and remaining water; stir well.

Bring chicken mixture to a boil; stir in flour mixture. Reduce heat and simmer uncovered 35 minutes.

Combine remaining 1 cup flour and baking powder. Add milk, stirring just until dry ingredients are moistened.

Drop batter by teaspoonfuls into boiling broth; cover. Reduce heat and simmer 15 minutes or until dumplings are tender.

Champagne Chicken

3 chicken breasts, deboned, skinned
2 tbsp. butter
2 tbsp. olive oil
1/4 c. dry champagne
1/2 c. heavy cream
1 tbsp. dry tarragon
1/8 tsp. salt
1/8 tsp. pepper

Cut chicken into 1/4-inch wide slices. Melt the butter and olive oil in a large heavy skillet. Sauté the chicken for 4 to 5 minutes.

Remove the chicken and keep warm. Deglaze the pan with the champagne. Add the cream to the pan.

Add the tarragon and reduce the sauce for two minutes. Put the chicken back into the pan, add salt and pepper and bring just to a simmer.

Remove to serving platter.

Serve hot with fresh vegetables or rice.

Chicken And Sweet Potatoes

2 c. sweet potatoes, cooked, mashed
2 tbsp. brown sugar
1/2 tsp. ground cinnamon
1/8 tsp. ground nutmeg
1/3 c. evaporated milk
1/4 c. chicken broth
1/4 c. onion, minced
8 oz. can water chestnuts, drained, sliced
10 oz. cream of chicken soup
3 c. chicken, cubed
3 tbsp. water

Preheat oven to 350°F.

In a bowl, combine sweet potatoes, brown sugar, cinnamon, nutmeg, and milk. Spread mixture around the inside edge of a round 10-inch casserole, forming a ring.

In a non-stick skillet, heat broth over low heat. Add onion and water chestnuts; cook until tender. Add soup, chicken, and 3 tablespoons water. Cook over medium heat until hot, stirring occasionally.

Spoon chicken mixture into center of sweet potato ring in casserole.

Bake uncovered, 30 minutes or until bubbling.

Holiday Baked Oysters

4 c. firm white bread (Italian, French or sourdough)
1/2 c. butter, divided
salt and cayenne pepper
1 pt. raw oysters, well drained
1 tbsp. lemon juice
1 onion, grated
1/2 c. whipping cream
paprika

Remove the crusts from the bread. Cut the bread into quarter-inch cubes. In a large skillet, melt half the butter.

Add 2 cups of bread cubes and toss over LOW HEAT until they are golden brown. Sprinkle the cubes lightly with salt and cayenne, stirring constantly. Brown the remaining cubes in the remaining butter.

Sprinkle again with the cayenne and the salt. Cover the bottom of a 2-quart baking dish with 1/3 of the bread cubes. Top the bread evenly with half the oysters. Sprinkle with salt and cayenne, half the lemon juice and half the onion.

Cover with 1/3 of the bread cubes and sprinkle with salt, cayenne, the rest of the lemon juice and the onion. Pour in the cream, and top with the last third of the bread cubes. Sprinkle with paprika.

Bake at 325°F for 25–35 minutes.

Stuffings & Gravies

Combine:
To stir together two or more ingredients.

Cream:
To beat a mixture with a spoon or electric mixer until it is smooth, light, fluffy, and nearly twice its original volume.

Wild Rice Stuffing

2 14 1/2 oz. cans chicken broth
2/3 c. wild rice
1 tsp. salt
1/2 tsp. dried thyme
1 1/2 c. water
2 tbsp. vegetable oil, divided
4 carrots, sliced
2 celery stalks, sliced
1 onion, chopped
10 oz. mushrooms, sliced
1 1/2 c. long-grain rice
1/4 c. parsley, chopped

In large saucepan over high heat, heat chicken broth, wild rice, salt, thyme, and water to boiling. Reduce heat to low; cover and simmer 35 minutes.

Meanwhile, in non-stick 10-inch skillet, over medium-high heat, heat 1 tablespoon vegetable oil. Add carrots, celery, and onion and cook until tender-crisp, stirring occasionally. Remove vegetable mixture to bowl.

In same skillet, add remaining tablespoon vegetable oil and cook mushrooms until golden brown and all liquid evaporates.

Stir long-grain rice, vegetable mixture, and mushrooms into wild rice. Heat to boiling, then reduce heat to low; cover and simmer 20 minutes longer or until all liquid is absorbed and rice is tender.

Stir in chopped parsley.

Almond Sausage Stuffing

1 c. slivered almonds, roasted
1 lb. pork sausage
8 c. dry bread cubes
2 c. celery, thinly sliced
1 c. onions, chopped
8 oz. mushrooms, sliced
1 tsp. poultry seasoning
1/2 c. water
1 egg, slightly beaten

To roast the almonds, place in oiled pan over medium heat, stirring frequently until golden.

Brown sausage in skillet, breaking it apart as it cooks. Drain sausage, reserving drippings. Add sausage to bread cubes. Add the celery, onions, and mushrooms to the drippings in the skillet, cooking until tender-crisp. Stir into sausage mixture along with the almonds and poultry seasoning. Add water and egg. Toss until mixed thoroughly. Do not stuff bird until ready to place in oven. Leftover dressing should be cooked in casserole dish for 30–45 minutes.

Brown Sauce

2 tbsp. margarine
1 c. beef stock
1 slice onion
salt and pepper to taste
2 tbsp. flour

Heat margarine over low heat until melted. Cook and stir onion in margarine until browned. Discard onion. Stir in flour, cooking over low heat, stirring constantly, until flour is a deep brown. Remove from heat. Stir in broth. Heat to boiling, stirring constantly. Boil and stir 1 minute, then add salt and pepper.

Turkey Gravy

turkey giblets and neck
water
salt
celery leaves
1 onion, sliced
1/2 c. skimmed turkey fat
1/2 c. flour
2 c. pan juices (add water if necessary
   to make 2 cups)
1 c. half-and-half
4 tbsp. brandy

Remove the liver and set aside. In a saucepan, cover the giblets and neck with lightly salted cold water. Add a few celery leaves and onion slices. Cover and simmer 1 hour.

Add the liver and simmer 20–30 minutes more. Remove and chop the giblets. Discard the neck.

Combine the turkey fat with flour in a saucepan over heat. Whisk in the broth and juices. Whisk in half-and-half. Stir in giblets.

Cook until thick and bubbly, then continue to cook 1 minute more. Stir in brandy. Serve over sliced turkey.

Turkey with Oyster Stuffing

Stuffing:
8 c. cornbread, crumbled
5 scallions, minced (include tops)
10 mushrooms, chopped
1 c. pecans, coarsely chopped
18 oysters, drained, chopped (reserve liquid)
turkey giblets, cooked, chopped
   (reserve liquid)
1 egg
1 garlic clove, crushed
2 tbsp. parsley, minced
1/4 tsp. ground pepper
2 1/2 tsp. salt
1 (12–14 lb.) turkey
1/2 c. butter, melted, divided

Preheat oven to 325°F.

Mix all stuffing ingredients (except the reserved liquids) together thoroughly. Stuff both the neck and body cavities of the turkey.

Wrap the remaining stuffing in aluminum foil. Skewer the openings shut; truss, and place the turkey, breast down, on a poultry rack in a large roasting pan.

Place the foil-wrapped stuffing in the bottom of the pan. Rub the bird generously with 1/4 cup softened butter.

To make the basting liquid, combine the reserved oyster liquid, giblet cooking liquid, and 1/4 cup melted butter.

Roast the turkey, uncovered, basting every 20 minutes. After 1 1/2 hours of roasting, turn the turkey breast side up. Allow about 30 minutes per pound for roasting the turkey, or follow the directions for cooking time and temperatures given on the package.

Sage Dressing

3 c. onions, chopped
3 c. celery, chopped
1 c. butter, melted, divided
16 slices white bread, dried and broken into small pieces
3 tbsp. dried sage
1 c. fresh parsley, minced
2 tsp. salt, or to taste
1 tsp. ground black pepper
2 c. turkey broth

In a skillet, cook the onions and celery in 4 tablespoons of butter over moderate heat until they are soft but not browned. In a large bowl, combine the dried bread pieces, sage, parsley, salt, and pepper. Add the onion and celery mixture and remaining melted butter. Toss until well mixed. Add broth slowly, a little at a time, while tossing mixture to moisten thoroughly. Add more sage, onions, or celery to taste. Dressing may be used to stuff a turkey or it may be cooked separately in a large pan at 350°F for 1 hour.

Sausage and Wild Rice Stuffing

1/3 c. onion, minced
1/2 c. butter
1 c. mushrooms, chopped
1/2 c. sausage
1 c. wild rice, cooked
2 tbsp. parsley, minced
1/2 tsp. sage
salt and pepper to taste

Sauté onion in butter. Add chopped mushrooms and sausage; fry until done. Combine wild rice, sausage mixture, parsley, sage, salt, and pepper. Makes a wonderful stuffing for chicken, turkey, duck, or squab.

Madeira Gravy

1 c. Madeira wine
pan juices from a roasted turkey
1 c. chicken broth
1/8 tsp. pepper
1/8 tsp. dried thyme

Boil wine, uncovered, in a small saucepan until reduced by half. Strain the pan juices into a 2-cup glass measure, gently pressing on the solids to extract all of the liquid. Let the juices rest for a few minutes, then skim away the grease. Add enough chicken broth to make 1 1/2 cups of liquid. Add the juice-broth mixture to the reduced wine, along with the pepper and thyme. Boil for 1–2 minutes. Remove from heat and serve with turkey.

Sweet and Sour Sauce

1/2 c. brown sugar, firmly packed
1 1/2 c. pineapple juice
2 tbsp. cornstarch
2 tbsp. soy sauce
1/2 c. cider vinegar

Combine all ingredients in a saucepan and cook over medium heat, stirring until it thickens and becomes clear. Makes an excellent sauce for poultry.

Apple and Bacon Cornbread Stuffing

Cornbread:

1 1/2 c. all-purpose flour
1 c. yellow cornmeal
1/4 c. sugar
1 tbsp. baking powder
1 tsp. salt
2 eggs
3/4 c. milk
1/2 c. butter, melted

Stuffing:

3/4 lb. bacon, cut into 1-inch pieces
2 tbsp. butter
3 apples, cored and cut into 1-inch pieces
3 ribs celery, chopped
6 scallions, chopped
1 tbsp. fresh parsley, chopped
2 tsp. dried marjoram
1 tsp. dried sage
1/2 tsp. salt
1/2 tsp. pepper
2 eggs
1 3/4 c. chicken broth

Preheat oven to 400°F. Grease a 9-inch square baking pan.

For cornbread, combine the flour, cornmeal, sugar, baking powder, and salt. Make a well in center of the dry ingredients. Add the eggs, milk, and melted butter. Stir until just combined. Spoon batter into prepared pan. Bake for 20–25 minutes, or until a toothpick inserted in the center comes out clean. Cool on a wire rack for 10 minutes. Remove from pan and cut into 1-inch cubes. Place on an ungreased baking sheet. Bake 30 minutes, or until the cubes are toasted; set aside.

For stuffing, cook the bacon in a large skillet over medium heat until crisp. With a slotted spoon, remove bacon to paper towels. Reserve 2 tablespoons of the drippings.

In the same skillet, over medium heat, melt butter in the reserved drippings. Add apples and celery. Cook for 15 minutes, or until tender. Stir in the scallions, parsley, marjoram, sage, salt, and pepper; set aside.

In medium bowl, whisk together eggs and broth.

In a large bowl, combine the cornbread cubes, bacon, and apple mixture. Stir in the broth mixture until just combined. Fill the turkey cavities with stuffing. Spoon the remaining stuffing into a greased, 2-quart casserole. Cover and put in the oven to heat 30 minutes before turkey is done.

Turkey Giblet Gravy

1/4 c. pan drippings from a roasted turkey
1/4 c. flour
1 c. water
2 c. turkey stock
turkey giblets, cooked and chopped
salt
pepper

Pour off all turkey fat from the roasting pan into a glass measuring cup. Measure and return 1/4 cup to pan. Sprinkle flour into the fat. Cook, stirring constantly, for 2–3 minutes over low heat. Add water and turkey stock. Cook, stirring and scraping up browned bits in pan with a wooden spoon, until gravy thickens and bubbles. Strain gravy into a saucepan. Add giblets. Season with salt and pepper.

Blender Gravy

3 tbsp. meat drippings
2 c. milk
1/4 c. all-purpose flour
salt
pepper

Remove the meat to a hot platter. Leaving the crusty bits of meat in the pan, pour the meat juices and fat into a large measuring cup.

Skim off the fat, reserving 3 tablespoons. Add milk, then flour, to blender container, blending until the liquid is smooth.

Return the blended gravy to the pan and cook the mixture quickly, stirring constantly, until the gravy is thick and bubbly. Season to taste with salt and pepper.

If desired, add a few drops of Kitchen Bouquet for color.

Mint Sauce

3 c. mint leaves, stems removed
3 tsp. sugar
4 tbsp. lemon juice
1 tsp. olive oil

Wash the mint leaves, sprinkle them with sugar and chop finely. Heat the lemon juice, add oil, and pour it over the mint. Add more sugar if you think the sauce is too sharp. Serve hot or cold with roasted lamb or other meat.

Basting Sauce For Roast

2 tsp. salt
2 tsp. dry mustard
1 tsp. pepper
1/2 tsp. garlic salt
2 tbsp. mayonnaise
2 tsp. onion salt
2 tbsp. vinegar
2 tsp. celery salt
2 tbsp. Kitchen Bouquet

Mix together all ingredients. Place unseasoned roast in roaster with one inch water. Cover and cook until 30 minutes before desired doneness. Add sauce and baste. Continue to cook, covered, until tender. Thicken liquid with flour and serve with roast.

Béarnaise Sauce

2 tbsp. white wine vinegar
1/4 c. dry white wine
2 shallots, minced
2 tbsp. tarragon leaves, chopped
3 egg yolks
1/3 c. butter
salt and pepper to taste

Combine vinegar, wine, shallots and tarragon in small glass bowl. Microwave, uncovered, at high for 1 to 2 minutes or until boiling. Set aside to cool to lukewarm. Strain mixture into a separate small bowl; whisk in egg yolks. Melt butter, but do not boil. Whisk egg yolk mixture into butter.

Microwave, uncovered, at medium, 30 to 90 seconds. Whisk every 15 seconds. Cook only until mixture starts to thicken. Season to taste with salt and pepper.

Vegetables & Side Dishes

Cut In:
To mix a solid fat, such as butter, with dry ingredients using a pastry cutter, food processor, or two knives.

Dough:
A thick mixture of flour and liquid that is combined with other ingredients to make recipes such as cookies or bread.

Acorn Squash with Cranberry Stuffing

4 small acorn squash
salt
8 tbsp. butter
8 tbsp. honey
16 oz. whole berry cranberry sauce

Wash and dry the squash. Cook the squash, uncovered, in the microwave for 15 minutes, or until soft to the touch. Let stand 5 minutes. Slice each in half and remove the seeds. Place the squash, cut side up, in a shallow microwave-safe baking dish. Sprinkle with salt. Place 1 tablespoon butter and 1 tablespoon honey into each half. Microwave, uncovered, for 4 minutes, or until the butter has melted.

With a brush or spoon, spread the honey-butter mixture over the cut surfaces of the squash. Place a spoonful of cranberry sauce into each squash half. Serve as is, or warm in the microwave until the cranberry sauce is hot.

Cauliflower au Gratin

6 tbsp. butter
2 cloves garlic, minced
4 oz. cooked ham, chopped
6 oz. cauliflower, broken into florets
2 tbsp. all-purpose flour
1 1/2 c. whipping cream
1/4 tsp. salt
1/8 tsp. pepper
pinch cayenne pepper
1 1/2 c. Swiss cheese, shredded
2 tbsp. fresh parsley, chopped

Melt butter in a large skillet. Sauté garlic and ham for 2 minutes. Add cauliflower and cook until tender-crisp.

Combine flour and cream; stir into the skillet and blend well. Add salt, pepper, and cayenne pepper. Cook and stir until thickened and bubbly; then cook and stir 1 minute more.

Pour into a 2-quart baking dish. Sprinkle with cheese. Place under a preheated broiler until lightly browned, about 2–4 minutes. Sprinkle with parsley. Serve immediately.

Holiday Coleslaw

2 c. green cabbage, shredded
2 c. red cabbage, shredded
1 green pepper, grated
1 red pepper, grated
1 red onion, grated
2 carrots, grated
1 c. mayonnaise
1/2 c. oil & vinegar dressing

Toss vegetables in a glass bowl. Combine mayonnaise and dressing. Pour over vegetables. Toss gently. Cover and chill overnight.

Corn Vegetable Medley

1 can golden corn soup
1/2 c. milk
2 c. broccoli florets
1 c. carrots, sliced
1 c. cauliflower florets
1/2 c. cheddar cheese, shredded

In a saucepan, heat the soup and milk to boiling, stirring often. Stir in vegetables and return to a boil. Cover and cook over low heat, stirring often, for 20 minutes, or until vegetables are tender. Stir in cheese and heat through. Serve immediately.

Crispy String Beans

2 c. plus 1 tbsp. vegetable oil, divided
3/4 lb. string beans, trimmed
1 tbsp. garlic, minced
2 tbsp. soy sauce
1/2 tbsp. sherry
1/2 tbsp. sugar
4 tbsp. chicken broth
1/2 tbsp. sesame oil
1 tbsp. scallions, minced

Heat 2 cups vegetable oil in a wok and add the beans. Fry for 1 minute, or until soft. Drain.

In a sauté pan, heat the remaining oil. Add the beans, garlic, soy sauce, sherry, sugar, and broth. Add the sesame oil and scallions, swirling to heat through. Beans should be extremely crisp.

Sweet Garden Peas with Mint

3 large lettuce leaves, shredded
2 tbsp. scallions, minced
1 tsp. butter
1/2 tsp. salt
1/4 tsp. pepper
30 oz. frozen peas, thawed
1/2 c. water
2 tbsp. fresh mint, shredded

Place the lettuce in a heavy saucepan. Add the scallions, butter, salt, and pepper. Cover and cook on high until steam starts to rise.

Add the peas and water. Cover again, and bring to a boil. Reduce heat and simmer 10–15 minutes, or until peas are tender but still retain bright color.

Stir in mint, cover, and steam for 1 minute. Serve immediately.

Cheesy Garlic Potatoes

1/4 c. butter, melted
7 c. potatoes, thinly sliced
1 tsp. garlic, minced
1/4 c. onion, minced
1 tsp. salt
1/2 tsp. white pepper
1 c. milk
1 c. Swiss cheese, grated
1 egg

Preheat oven to 425°F.

Combine butter, potatoes, garlic, onion, salt, and pepper in a bowl and mix well. Place in a baking dish. Cover and bake for 10 minutes.

In a small saucepan, scald the milk, then add it to the potatoes. Return the potatoes to the oven and bake, uncovered, for an additional 20 minutes.

Add the cheese and egg to the potatoes in the baking dish, mixing well. Bake for another 10–15 minutes, or until the top is browned.

Cranberry Fruit Salad

2 pkg. cherry gelatin
2 c. boiling water
12 oz. cranberries, fresh or frozen
1 large apple, peeled and chopped
1 large orange, peeled, chopped and seeded
1 piece of orange peel (1-inch)
20 oz. pineapple, undrained, crushed, unsweetened

In a bowl, dissolve gelatin in water. Stir in all remaining ingredients. Process in small batches in a blender until coarsely chopped. Pour into a 13 x 9 x 2-inch dish and chill until set.

Glazed Pearl Onions

16 oz. frozen pearl onions
2 tbsp. vegetable oil
3 tbsp. sugar
1 1/2 c. beef stock
4 tbsp. red wine vinegar
salt and pepper to taste

Rinse the onions in a colander, just enough to separate them and remove the extra ice. Blot them on paper towels.

In a large, heavy skillet, heat the oil over high heat. When it is hot, add the onions and sugar. Cook for 5 minutes, shaking often, until the onions are lightly colored. Add the beef stock. Reduce heat to medium, and continue cooking until the liquid is almost completely evaporated, about 20–25 minutes. Stir in the vinegar, cook for 30 seconds. Season with salt and pepper to taste. Serve immediately.

Elegant Stuffed Pumpkin

1 (5-lb.) pumpkin
2 1/2 c. brown rice, cooked
2 c. dry bread, crumbled
1 onion, chopped
3/4 c. celery, chopped
2 tart apples, unpeeled and chopped
1 c. chestnuts, roasted
1 tsp. sage
1 tsp. marjoram
1 tsp. oregano
1 1/2 c. vegetable stock
1/2 c. butter, melted
1/2 tsp. soy sauce
salt to taste

Preheat oven to 325°F.

Cut off the top of the pumpkin to make a lid. Remove the seeds and scrape the stringy pulp; set aside.

Combine the rice, bread, onion, celery, apples, chestnuts, sage, marjoram, and oregano in a large bowl and mix well. Add the vegetable stock and butter. Mix well, adding soy sauce and salt. Stuffing should be moist but not wet.

Loosely pack the stuffing into the pumpkin. Replace the lid and place the pumpkin on an oiled cookie sheet. Bake for 1 1/2 hours, or until a fork pushes easily through the pumpkin.

Transfer the pumpkin to a casserole dish and serve, scooping out some of the tender pumpkin flesh with each serving of stuffing.

Winter Squash with Cranberries

1 1/2 c. squash, cooked
1 egg, beaten
1/2 c. cranberries, chopped
1/2 tsp. salt
1/8 tsp. pepper
1 tbsp. butter, melted
1/8 tsp. nutmeg

Preheat oven to 400°F.

Combine the cooked squash and egg. Stir in the cranberries, salt, and pepper. Turn into a 1 1/2-quart casserole dish. Drizzle melted butter over top. Sprinkle with nutmeg. Bake 35–40 minutes.

Homestyle Spinach

2 lb. spinach
1 tsp. salt
1/4 c. olive oil
1/4 tsp. sugar
2 garlic cloves, minced
2 tbsp. lemon juice
3 tbsp. Parmesan cheese, freshly grated

Wash the spinach and cook with salt for not more than 5 minutes. Coarsely chop the spinach.

Heat the olive oil in a skillet. Add the spinach, sugar, and garlic. Reduce heat to simmer, slowly stirring the spinach to coat well with oil. Sprinkle with lemon juice and mix thoroughly. Cover and cook 15 minutes. During the last 5 minutes of cooking, stir in the cheese until evenly distributed. Serve hot.

Maple-Glazed Carrots

8 medium carrots
1/2 c. fresh orange juice
rind of 1 orange, grated
3 tbsp. maple syrup
1/8 tsp. nutmeg
3 tbsp. butter

Peel the carrots and cut them into sticks.

Pour the orange juice into a 4-cup, microwave-safe dish. Heat on high for 1 minute. Add the carrots and orange rind, stirring to coat. Cover and microwave on high for 8–9 minutes. Stir again, then add the remaining ingredients. Microwave, uncovered, on high for 2 minutes. Stir, then check for doneness. If necessary, cook at additional 1 minute intervals until desired doneness is reached.

Parmesan Asparagus Spears

1 tbsp. balsamic vinegar
1 tsp. olive oil
1 tsp. Dijon mustard
water
1 tsp. salt, divided
2 1/2 lb. asparagus spears
3 tbsp. Parmesan cheese, grated

Stir together the vinegar, oil, and mustard in a large bowl; set aside.

Heat 2 inches of water and 1/2 teaspoon salt to boiling in a large, deep skillet.

Slice off the tough lower stems of the asparagus spears.

Rinse the spears and place half of them in the boiling water.

Cover and cook for 5–6 minutes, or just until tender-crisp. Using tongs, transfer the asparagus to the bowl with the vinegar mixture.

Pour out the cooking liquid. Prepare a fresh pot with 2 inches of water and the remaining 1/2 teaspoon of salt.

Bring to a boil and cook the remaining asparagus.

Transfer cooked asparagus to the vinegar mixture. Toss gently until spears are evenly coated.

Place asparagus on a serving plate. Sprinkle evenly with cheese, and serve.

Red and Green Potato Salad

3 lb. red-skin potatoes, diced
1 red onion, cut into thin rings
3 tbsp. parsley, minced
Juice of 1/2 lemon
1/3 c. olive oil
1 green pepper, cut into thin rings
salt and pepper to taste

Boil potatoes in their jackets until barely tender. Cool enough to handle and dice while still warm.

Place potatoes in a large salad bowl along with onion rings and green pepper; mix well. Add parsley and lemon juice; carefully toss again. Drizzle oil over the vegetables and season to taste with salt and pepper. Toss and set aside for several hours for salad ingredients to mellow.

If refrigerated, bring to room temperature before serving.

Baked Carrots

18 small carrots
1/3 c. butter
1/2 c. sugar
1 tsp. salt
1/3 tsp. cinnamon
1/3 c. boiling water

Scrape or pare carrots and place in casserole. Cream butter, sugar, salt and cinnamon together. Add water and blend well. Pour over carrots, cover and bake in moderate 350°F oven for 1 1/2 hours.

Braised Red Cabbage With Currants

1 tbsp. whole caraway seeds
2 tsp. dry red wine
1 red or yellow onion, thinly sliced
1/4 tsp. salt
1 red cabbage, thinly sliced
1/2 c. currants
2 tbsp. red wine vinegar
2/3 c. apple juice

Toast caraway seeds in a roaster oven or frying pan until they smell nutty, about one minute. In a large pot, heat wine. Add onion and salt, and sauté for five minutes, until onion wilts and smells very sweet. Add red cabbage and sauté over medium-low heat until it wilts a little, about 5 minutes. (Add water as needed to prevent sticking.) Add caraway seeds and currants.

Mix vinegar and apple juice; pour over the cabbage and mix well. Preheat oven to 375°F. Lightly oil a casserole dish and spoon the cabbage and liquid into it. Cover and bake for 45 to 60 minutes.

Roasted Sweet Corn

1/4 pound bacon
15 ears sweet corn
1 cup water

Fry bacon and reserve drippings. Cut corn kernels off the cob with a sharp knife. Next, with a dull knife, scrape off the pulp. In a large pan, mix corn, bacon drippings, water, and salt to taste. Stir well. Bake at 375°F for 30 minutes.

Brussels Sprouts In Mustard Sauce

10 oz. Brussels sprouts, frozen
1 1/2 c. chicken broth, divided
1 tsp. canola oil
2 tbsp. green onion, chopped
1 tsp. Dijon mustard
1/2 tsp. pepper
1 tbsp. cornstarch
1/2 c. evaporated milk

Cook Brussels sprouts in 1/2 cup of chicken broth; cover and set aside. Spray a small skillet with vegetable cooking spray and add the oil. Sauté onion in the oil. Remove from heat and slowly add the remaining cup of chicken broth. Stir in mustard and pepper. Return to heat. Dissolve the cornstarch in the milk, then add to skillet mixture. Stirring constantly, cook until sauce is smooth and thickened, about 5 minutes. Pour mustard sauce over cooked Brussels sprouts and stir to coat.

Butter Pecan Squash

1 1/2 lb. butternut squash
1/2 c. boiling water
3 tbsp. butter
1 tbsp. brown sugar
1/2 tsp. salt
1/2 c. pecans, coarsely chopped
2 tbsp. maple syrup

Prepare squash by scooping seeds and stringy portion; pare and cut into 3/4-inch cubes. In a medium saucepan, bring squash and water to a boil; cover and cook rapidly until squash is tender (about 10 minutes). Drain and mash with butter, sugar, and salt. Turn into a casserole dish; sprinkle with pecans and maple syrup. Broil until pecans are lightly browned.

Broiled Eggplant With Walnut Sauce

Walnut Sauce:
1 c. walnuts, coarsely chopped
1 garlic clove, minced
1/4 c. fresh bread crumbs
1 1/2 c. boiling water
3 tsp. olive oil
1/4 tsp. fennel seeds, crushed
salt and pepper

Eggplant:
light olive oil
eggplant, sliced 1/2-inch thick
freshly ground pepper
parsley, left in sprigs

Walnut Sauce:
Put the walnuts, garlic and bread crumbs in a food processor and process briefly until everything is the texture of fine crumbs. With the motor running, gradually pour in about 1 cup of the water. Stop and scrape down the sides, then add enough water until it is the consistency you want. (It will thicken somewhat as it sits.) Stir in the oil and fennel seeds. Season to taste with salt and pepper.

Eggplant:
Preheat broiler. Brush sides of the eggplant generously with oil. Place 3 inches from heat source and broil until golden brown. Turn rounds over and broil until nicely colored and tender. If eggplant looks dry, brush a little more oil over the top. Set broiled eggplants on a platter and spoon walnut sauce over the tops. Season with pepper. Serve hot or slightly cooled. Garnish dish with parsley sprigs.

Pecan Chicken and Rice

3/4 c. wild rice
4 1/2 c. chicken broth, divided
1 tbsp. butter
1 c. long grain rice
1/2 c. parsley, chopped
3/4 c. pecans, toasted, chopped

Rinse rice and combine with 2 1/2 cups of chicken broth. Heat to boiling. Cover; reduce heat and simmer 30 minutes. Drain excess broth; set aside. Heat remaining 2 cups of broth and butter to boiling. Add long grain rice, reduce heat, simmer, covered, 15 minutes. Combine rices. Toss with parsley and pecans.

Grapefruit Sweet Potatoes

1 3/4 lb. sweet potatoes
1 large grapefruit
3 tbsp. unsalted butter
1/3 c. light brown sugar, firmly packed
1/4 tsp. salt
2 eggs, well beaten

Preheat oven to 375°F.

Put the potatoes, unpeeled, in a large saucepan and cover with water. With a swivel-blade vegetable peeler, peel the yellow zest from the grapefruit and put it in with the potatoes. Bring to a boil, reduce the heat and simmer until the sweet potatoes are just fork-tender, about 20 minutes.

Meanwhile, with a long-pronged fork or tongs, dip the grapefruit into the boiling potato water and blanch, turning constantly, for 30 seconds. Rinse the grapefruit briefly under cold running water to cool and peel off the white pith. Section the grapefruit and peel off the membranes over a bowl to catch the juice. Reserve all the juice and pulp; discard seeds.

When the sweet potatoes are done, drain and allow to cool; discard the grapefruit zest. Peel the potatoes and put them into a food processor along with the grapefruit pulp and juice, butter, brown sugar and salt. Puree until smooth. Add eggs and mix to blend.

Pour the sweet potato mixture into a well buttered, 6-cup soufflé dish. Place in a pan of hot water and bake for 45 minutes, or until the center is set.

Vegetable Hash

2 medium potatoes, scrubbed,
  quartered, and thinly sliced
1 lb. mixed greens
2 tbsp. olive oil
2 small dried red chilies, seeds removed,
  torn into pieces
2 medium fresh tomatoes, chopped
2 garlic cloves, minced
salt and pepper to taste
1/2 c. hard cheese, freshly grated
1 tbsp. extra-virgin olive oil

Boil the potatoes until tender. Remove from water, reserving liquid. Chop the greens, removing tough stems. Cook the greens until done in the potato water. Warm the olive oil in a wide pan and add the chilies. When oil is hot, add potatoes, stir well and cook for two minutes. Add greens, tomatoes, and garlic. Continue cooking 5 minutes, breaking up the potatoes and working everything together. Taste for salt, add pepper and cheese, and serve with a bit of extra-virgin olive oil threaded over the top.

Casseroles

Dredge:
To coat, usually with flour.

Drizzle:
To pour a liquid, such as butter, over food in a thin stream.

Dust:
To lightly sprinkle an ingredient, such as confectioners' sugar, over a food.

Apple-Squash Casserole

1 medium butternut squash, strings and seed removed, thinly sliced
4 medium baking apples, peeled and thinly sliced
3 tbsp. brown sugar, firmly packed
1 tsp. cinnamon
1/2 tsp. nutmeg
1/2 tsp. cloves
1/2 tsp. ginger
1/2 c. walnuts, chopped
4 tbsp. butter, cut into pieces

Preheat oven to 350°F.

Butter a casserole dish. Place half of the squash slices in the bottom of the dish. Top with half of the apple slices.

In a small bowl, combine the brown sugar, cinnamon, nutmeg, cloves, ginger, and nuts. Dot the apples with 2 tablespoons butter and sprinkle with half of the spice mixture. Layer on the remaining squash and apples, ending with the spices. Dot with remaining butter. Bake, covered, for 45–60 minutes, or until tender.

Broccoli Casserole

1 bunch fresh broccoli, cooked
1 can (10 oz.) cream of mushroom soup
1/2 c. cheddar cheese, grated
3/4 c. milk
1 egg, beaten
3/4 c. mayonnaise
3/4 c. cracker crumbs
1 tbsp. butter, melted

Preheat oven to 350°F.

Place the cooked broccoli in a casserole dish. Mix together the soup, cheese, milk, egg, and mayonnaise. Pour over the broccoli. Combine the cracker crumbs and butter, mixing well. Sprinkle over the broccoli. Bake for 35 minutes, or until the top is browned.

Artichoke Spinach Casserole

1 jar (8 oz.) marinated artichoke hearts, drained (reserve liquid)
20 oz. spinach, cooked, drained, and squeezed dry
8 oz. cream cheese, softened
1/2 c. Parmesan cheese, grated
2 tbsp. butter, softened

Preheat oven to 350°F.

Spread the artichoke hearts in the bottom of a buttered casserole dish. Top with spinach. Cream together the cream cheese, Parmesan, and butter. Spread mixture evenly over the spinach. Bake, covered, for 30 minutes. Remove cover and bake for an additional 10 minutes. Serve immediately.

Baked Green Tomato Casserole

8 large green tomatoes
salt and pepper
1 c. brown sugar
1 1/2 c. cracker crumbs
1 stick butter

Cut tomatoes in half and arrange in an oiled, shallow casserole. Season with salt and pepper and spread each with a tablespoon of sugar. Cover with crumbs and dot with butter. Bake at 350°F until tender but still firm, about 30 minutes.

Christmas Potato Casserole

1 1/2 lb. potatoes, peeled
1/3 c. water
2 tbsp. butter
1 medium onion
1/2 c. bell pepper, chopped
2 oz. pimento, diced
1/2 tsp. salt
1/4 tsp. pepper
1/2 c. cheddar cheese, shredded
3 slices bacon, cooked and crumbled

Preheat oven to 375°F. Combine potatoes and water in a 2-quart, microwave-safe casserole dish. Cover and microwave on high for 8–10 minutes, or until potatoes are tender, stirring after 4 minutes. Drain. Add the butter, stirring until it melts. Add the onion, bell pepper, pimento, salt, and pepper, stirring to combine. Bake for 25 minutes. Sprinkle with cheese and bacon. Bake an additional 5 minutes, or until the cheese melts.

Papa John's Sweet Potato Casserole with Pecan Topping

3 lb. sweet potatoes
3/4 c. orange juice
2 large eggs
2 tbsp. butter, melted
2 tbsp. sugar
1/2 tsp. ground nutmeg
1 1/2 tsp. ground cinnamon

Pecan Topping:
1/2 c. all-purpose flour
1/4 c. plus 2 tbsp. brown sugar, firmly packed
1/2 tsp. ground cinnamon
1/4 c. butter, softened
1/2 c. pecans, chopped

Preheat oven to 350°F.

Place the sweet potatoes in a baking pan and bake 1 hour, or until all are tender. Butter an 8 x 8 x 2-inch glass baking dish.

Scrape all of the sweet potato pulp from skins. Using an electric mixer, mash the sweet potatoes. Add the orange juice, eggs, melted butter, sugar, nutmeg, and 1 1/2 teaspoons cinnamon. Beat until smooth. Spoon potatoes into prepared baking dish.

For the topping, combine the flour, brown sugar, and 1/2 teaspoon cinnamon in a medium bowl. Cut in the butter until the mixture resembles coarse crumbs. Mix in the pecans. Sprinkle mixture over the potatoes.

Bake at 350°F for 30 minutes.

Cabbage Roll Casserole

1 lb. ground beef
1 tbsp. vegetable oil
1 onion, thinly sliced
1/8 tsp. pepper
1/2 c. rice, uncooked
1 10 oz. can tomato soup
3 c. cabbage, shredded

Preheat oven to 325°F. Brown meat in oil, then add onion, salt and pepper. Drain. Add rice, mix well. Add soup and one can of water.

Put cabbage in baking dish; pour meat mixture over all, but do NOT stir. Bake, uncovered, for one hour.

Zucchini Stuffing Casserole

4 zucchini, cut into 2-inch thick slices
3/4 c. carrots, shredded
1/2 c. onion, chopped
6 tbsp. butter, divided
2 1/2 c. leftover stuffing, dry, divided
1 can condensed cream of chicken soup
1/2 c. sour cream

Preheat oven to 350°F.

Cook the zucchini in boiling water until tender. Drain; set aside. Sauté the carrots and onions in 4 tablespoons butter until tender. Remove from heat. Stir in 1 1/2 cups stuffing, soup, and sour cream. Gently stir in the zucchini. Turn into a casserole dish. Melt the remaining butter and combine it with the remaining stuffing; toss lightly to coat. Spoon mixture over the casserole. Bake, uncovered, for 30–40 minutes.

Yellow Squash Casserole

3 tbsp. butter
4 yellow summer squash, sliced
1 onion, chopped
4 oz. green chiles, chopped
10 saltine crackers, crushed
salt and pepper to taste
1 1/2 c. cheddar cheese, shredded

Preheat oven to 350°F.

In a skillet, melt the butter over medium heat. Add the squash and onion. Sauté until the vegetables are tender-crisp. Remove from heat. Stir in chiles, crackers, salt, and pepper. Spoon into a greased 1 1/2-quart casserole dish. Top with cheese. Bake for 15–20 minutes.

Onion Mushroom Casserole

5 c. Vidalia onions, sliced and peeled
1/4 c. butter, melted
1 1/2 c. fresh mushrooms, sliced
1/2 tsp. salt
3 oz. cream cheese
3 tsp. flour
1 1/2 c. milk
1/4 c. cheddar cheese, shredded
1/4 c. cracker crumbs

Preheat oven to 400°F.

Combine the onions with the butter, mushrooms, and salt. Simmer for 5 minutes in a medium saucepan. Add the cream cheese. When melted, add flour and milk. Heat through. Turn into a 2-quart, greased casserole dish.

Combine the cheese and cracker crumbs. Sprinkle over the casserole. Bake for 30 minutes.

Ham, Apples, and Sweet Potato Casserole

1 ham center slice
4 apples, quartered
3 medium sweet potatoes, sliced 1/4-inch thick
2 tbsp. sugar
3/4 c. hot water

Preheat oven to 350°F.

Brown the ham slightly on both sides and place in a baking dish. Spread the apple quarters and sweet potato slices over the ham and sprinkle with sugar. Add hot water. Cover and bake for 1 hour, or until tender. Baste occasionally while cooking. Remove cover for the last 15 minutes to brown.

Crabmeat Casserole

1 lb. lump crab meat
1/4 c. lemon juice
1/2 tsp. salt
1/4 c. butter
2 1/2 tbsp. all-purpose flour
1 1/2 c. milk
1/2 tsp. garlic salt
1/2 tsp. celery salt
1 tsp. parsley flakes
1 c. cheddar cheese, grated
2 tbsp. white wine
6 c. wild rice, cooked
6 oz. mushrooms, sliced

Preheat oven to 350°F.

Combine crab meat, lemon juice, and salt in a medium bowl. Refrigerate while preparing the sauce.

In a medium saucepan, melt the butter. Add the flour, stirring to blend. Cook for 1 minute.

Slowly add the milk, stirring constantly. Cook until the sauce thickens. Add the garlic salt, celery salt, parsley flakes, cheese, and wine. Stir until the cheese is melted and sauce is smooth.

Drain the crab meat, add it to the sauce and heat until bubbly.

Layer the rice in the bottom of a lightly oiled, 2-quart casserole dish. Pour the crab meat and sauce over the rice. Top with mushroom slices and bake for 30 minutes, or until lightly browned.

Christmas Ham and Noodle Casserole

1 pkg. (8 oz.) noodles
1 medium onion, chopped
1/2 bell pepper, chopped
1/2 lb. mushrooms
4 tbsp. butter
1 small can olives, chopped
1 1/2 c. tomatoes, fresh or canned
1 pt. sour cream
2 c. cooked ham, cubed
2 c. cheddar cheese, grated
salt and pepper to taste

Preheat oven to 325°F. Cook noodles in salted water; drain and set aside. Sauté the onion, bell pepper, and mushrooms in butter for 5 minutes. Add the remaining ingredients, stirring to blend. Add all to the noodles and stir to blend. Turn mixture into a 3-quart casserole dish. Bake for 30–40 minutes.

Green Bean And Onion Casserole

3 tbsp. butter
3 tbsp. flour
1 tbsp. prepared mustard
1/2 tsp. salt
1/4 tsp. hot sauce
16 oz. can green beans; reserve liquid
milk
16 oz. jar pearl onions, whole
1 c. bread cubes, buttered

Melt butter; add flour, stirring until smooth. Add mustard, salt, hot sauce, and bean liquid plus milk to make 1 1/2 cups; cook until thick. Add beans and drained onions. Place in a greased 1-quart casserole; border with buttered bread crumbs. Bake in preheated 375°F oven 30 minutes.

Chicken and Dumpling Casserole

1/2 c. onion, chopped
1/2 c. celery, chopped
2 garlic cloves, minced
1/4 c. butter
1/2 c. flour
2 tsp. sugar
1 tsp. salt
1 tsp. dried basil
1/2 tsp. pepper
4 c. chicken broth
10 oz. green peas, frozen
4 c. chicken, cooked, cubed

Dumplings:
2 c. buttermilk biscuit mix
2 tsp. dried basil
2/3 c. milk

In a large saucepan, sauté onion, celery and garlic in butter until tender. Add flour, sugar, salt, basil, pepper and broth; bring to a boil. Cook and stir for one minute; reduce heat. Add peas and cook for 5 minutes, stirring constantly.

Stir in cubed chicken. Pour into a greased 13 x 9 x 2-inch baking dish.

For dumplings, combine biscuit mix and basil in a bowl. Stir in milk with a fork until moistened.

Drop by tablespoonfuls onto casserole (12 dumplings). Bake, uncovered, at 350°F for 30 minutes. Cover and bake 10 minutes more or until dumplings are done.

Golden Crumb Broccoli

1 1/2 lb. fresh broccoli
1 can cream of mushroom soup
1/4 c. mayonnaise
1/4 c. cheddar cheese, shredded
1 tbsp. pimento, chopped
1 1/2 tsp. lemon juice
1/3 c. round cheese crackers, crushed

Cut broccoli into small pieces, enough to make about 6 cups. In saucepan, cook broccoli, uncovered, in small amount of boiling, salted water for 10 to 15 minutes; drain well. Turn into a 1 1/2-quart casserole.

Mix soup, mayonnaise, cheese, pimento, and lemon juice. Pour over broccoli. Top with crushed crackers. Bake uncovered, at 350°F for 35 minutes.

Tater Tot Casserole

2 lb. ground chuck
1 onion, chopped
salt and pepper to taste
10 3/4 oz. cream of mushroom soup
16 oz. cheddar cheese, shredded
12 oz. sour cream
1 large bag of Tater Tots
10 3/4 oz. cream of chicken soup

Brown ground chuck and chopped onion; season with salt and pepper. Drain. Layer other ingredients into baking dish. Top with large bag of Tater Tots. Bake at 350°F for 1 hour or until brown and heated through.

Leftover Solutions

Fold:
To gently combine two mixtures using a spatula in a light, circular motion.

Glaze:
To give food a shiny coating by applying a thin layer of syrup, beaten egg, or milk.

Turkey Broccoli Bake

2 bunches fresh broccoli, cut into florets
1 lb. leftover turkey
2 cans cream of mushroom soup
1 c. water
1 c. mayonnaise
3/4 tsp. curry powder
1/2 c. almonds, toasted, slivered

Preheat oven to 350°F.

Slightly steam broccoli florets. Place in a greased casserole dish and top with the turkey. In a separate bowl, combine the soup, water, mayonnaise, and curry powder. Pour over the casserole. Bake for 45 minutes. Garnish with almond slivers.

Turkey Meatloaf

1 tbsp. butter
1 large yellow onion, chopped
3/4 lb. mushrooms, chopped
1 clove garlic, chopped
2 tbsp. Italian salad dressing
1/2 tsp. hot sauce
1 large jar pasta sauce, divided
1 small can tomato paste
3 lb. ground turkey
1 c. seasoned bread crumbs, divided

Preheat oven to 425°F. In a large sauté pan, melt butter. Add onion, and sauté over medium-high heat until transparent. Add mushrooms, garlic, Italian dressing, hot sauce, and 3/4 of pasta sauce. Lower heat to medium-low and simmer for 5 minutes, stirring occasionally. Add tomato paste, stirring well. Simmer for another 5 minutes.

In a large bowl, combine onion-mushroom mixture with the ground turkey, blending well with a wooden spoon. Add 1/2 cup bread crumbs and stir well. Continue adding bread crumbs until mixture holds together but isn't dry. Be sure to mix well after each addition of crumbs. Mixture should hold together when the back of a spoon is pressed against it. Place mixture in an oven-safe pan and shape into a loaf. Bake for 1 hour. Pour remaining pasta sauce on top, spreading it over the entire loaf. Bake for an additional 30–45 minutes. Remove from oven and let stand for 5 minutes before serving.

Wild Mushroom and Turkey Pasta

1/2 stick butter
2 large Spanish onions, slivered
2 tbsp. brown sugar
4 oz. dried morel mushrooms, rehydrated
1 c. cooked turkey, cubed
1 tsp. fresh thyme, minced
1 1/2 lb. cheese-filled pasta
1/3 lb. fresh spinach
1 clove garlic, minced
1 small head radicchio, shredded
1/2 c. Parmesan cheese, grated
1/2 c. Gruyère cheese, grated
salt and pepper to taste

In a large frying pan, melt butter over medium heat. Add onions and brown sugar. Cook for 15 minutes, stirring frequently. Add mushrooms, turkey, and thyme. Cook 10 minutes more. Remove from heat; set aside. Cook pasta according to package directions. Toss with onion mixture. Add spinach, garlic, radicchio, Parmesan, and Gruyère, tossing to mix. Add salt and pepper to taste.

Turkey Broccoli Mushroom Bake

1 1/2 lb. broccoli
6 tbsp. butter, divided
1/4 c. flour
1/2 tsp. salt
1/4 tsp. pepper
2 c. milk
1 c. cheddar cheese, shredded
1/2 lb. mushrooms
2 tbsp. green bell pepper, chopped
1 c. cooked turkey, diced
additional shredded cheese
paprika

Preheat oven to 350°F.

Separate the broccoli stalks and cook them in 1 inch of boiling salted water for 3–5 minutes. Drain. Arrange the cooked broccoli in a greased, 9-inch square pan.

Melt 5 tablespoons butter and blend in the flour, salt, and pepper. Cook and stir until smooth. Remove from heat and stir in the milk. Return to heat and bring mixture to a boil. Boil for 1 minute, stirring constantly. Add cheese and remove from heat.

Sauté mushrooms in the remaining 1 tablespoon butter until tender. Add mushrooms along with bell peppers. Cook the sauce for 1 minute. Add turkey and pour all over the broccoli. Sprinkle with additional cheese and paprika.
Bake for 15–20 minutes.

Swiss Broccoli Pie

1 lb. fresh broccoli
2/3 c. onion, chopped
1/4 c. water
4 eggs, slightly beaten
1 1/4 c. milk
1/2 c. leftover turkey meat, shredded
2/3 c. Swiss cheese, shredded
1/8 tsp. pepper
1/8 tsp. ground nutmeg
1 tbsp. fresh parsley, minced
1/2 tsp. salt
1/8 tsp. hot sauce
1/3 c. Parmesan cheese, grated

Preheat oven to 350°F.

Trim the large leaves off the broccoli. Remove the tough ends of the lower stalks. Wash broccoli thoroughly. Cut the florets and stems into thin slices.

Combine broccoli, onion, and water in a saucepan. Cover and cook over medium heat for 6–8 minutes. Drain thoroughly, pressing out the moisture with paper towels.

In a separate bowl, combine all remaining ingredients except the Parmesan cheese. Stir in the vegetables and pour the mixture into a greased 10-inch pie plate.

Sprinkle with Parmesan cheese and bake for 30 minutes, or until set. Let stand 10 minutes before serving.

Turkey Pie with Biscuit Crust

Filling:
4 c. chicken broth
3 carrots, cut into 1/4-inch slices
3/4 lb. red potatoes, diced
2 ribs celery, diced
2 1/2 c. cooked turkey, cubed
1 onion, chopped
6 tbsp. unsalted butter
6 tbsp. flour
1/4 tsp. thyme
1/4 tsp. nutmeg
1/2 c. fresh parsley, minced
salt and pepper to taste

Biscuit Crust:
1 1/3 c. flour
1 1/2 tsp. baking powder
1/2 tsp. baking soda
1/2 tsp. salt
2 tbsp. unsalted butter, cut into small pieces
2 tbsp. shortening, cut into small pieces
1/3 c. cheddar cheese, grated
1 large egg
1/3 c. buttermilk

Egg Wash:
1 egg yolk
2 tbsp. milk

In a saucepan, bring the chicken broth to a boil. Add carrots, potatoes, and celery. Simmer for 10–15 minutes, or until the vegetables are tender.

Transfer vegetables to a bowl, reserving broth. Add turkey to the bowl. In another saucepan, cook onion in butter over low heat, stirring until softened. Add flour to make a roux.

Cook the roux, stirring continuously for 3 minutes. Add 3 cups broth in a stream, whisking constantly. Bring mixture to a boil, whisking continuously. Add the thyme and simmer, stirring occasionally, for 5 minutes. Stir in the nutmeg, parsley, salt and pepper to taste. Pour sauce over turkey and vegetables. Stir gently until mixture is combined. Transfer the mixture to a 2-quart baking dish.

Preheat oven to 450°F.

In a bowl, sift together the flour, baking powder, baking soda, and salt. Cut in the butter and shortening until mixture resembles coarse meal. Add cheese and toss.

Break egg into a measuring cup. Add enough buttermilk so that the total volume is 1/2 cup.

Beat with a fork. Add to flour mixture, stirring just until the mixture forms a dough. Shape the dough into a ball and turn it out on a lightly floured surface. Pat it out until it is 1/2-inch thick.

Cut into rounds using a 2-inch, fluted biscuit cutter, dipped in flour. Arrange rounds over the turkey mixture.

Beat the egg yolk with the milk. Brush tops of biscuits with the wash. Prick biscuits with a fork. Place on the middle rack of the oven.

Bake for 15–25 minutes or until the biscuits are puffed and golden and the filling is bubbling.

White Bean Turkey Chili

1/4 c. butter
1 c. onion, chopped
1 clove garlic, finely chopped
4 c. cooked turkey, cubed
3 c. turkey broth
2 cans (32 oz.) Great Northern beans
2 tbsp. cilantro
2 tsp. ground red chiles
1 tbsp. basil
1/4 tsp. ground cloves

Melt butter in a 4-quart Dutch oven. Add the onion and garlic. Cook, stirring constantly, until the onion is tender. Stir in the remaining ingredients. Heat to boiling. Reduce heat, cover and simmer for at least 1 hour, stirring occasionally. Serve with tortilla chips and shredded cheese.

Baked Turkey and Ham Hash

4 tbsp. butter
3 1/2 tbsp. flour
2 c. milk
1/2 c. turkey broth
2 c. cooked turkey, diced
1 c. cooked country ham, diced
1/4 c. fresh bread crumbs
1/4 c. cheddar cheese, crumbled
1 c. mozzarella cheese, shredded
2 tbsp. Madeira wine
4 eggs

Preheat oven to 350°F.

Melt the butter in a saucepan. Stir in the flour and cook for 2 minutes over low heat. Remove from heat and stir in the milk and turkey broth. Return to heat and stir mixture until it is thick and smooth. In a greased casserole, combine the turkey and ham, spreading the meats evenly over the bottom of the dish. Pour in half of the sauce, keeping the remaining sauce hot.

Combine bread crumbs, cheddar, mozzarella, and Madeira. Sprinkle mixture over top of casserole.

Bake for 25 minutes or until a crusty, light brown surface develops. Make 4 indentations on the surface of the casserole and carefully break an egg into each. Cover the eggs with the remaining sauce. Return to the oven for an additional 18 minutes or until the eggs have set.

Turkey Strata

1 c. turkey, cooked, diced
1 c. cheddar cheese, shredded, divided
1/4 c. green olives, sliced
4 c. bread cubes
1 c. milk
1/2 c. salad dressing
2 eggs

Combine turkey, 1/2 cup of cheese, and olives; mix lightly. Place 1/2 bread cubes in 8 x 8-inch baking dish; top with turkey mixture and remaining bread cubes. Combine all remaining ingredients except cheese; pour over bread. Refrigerate overnight.

Preheat oven to 375°F. Top with remaining cheese. Bake for 40 minutes or until set. Let stand 10 minutes before serving.

Turkey Enchiladas

1 can (10 oz.) enchilada sauce, divided
1 can (15.5 oz.) dark red kidney beans,
   drained and rinsed
8 (6-inch) corn tortillas
1 c. cooked turkey, shredded
3/4 c. Mexican-style cheese,
   shredded, divided

Preheat oven to 300°F.

Spray a 13 x 9-inch baking dish with non-stick cooking spray. Also spray a sheet of aluminum foil cut slightly larger than the baking dish. Set aside. Reserve 1/3 cup of enchilada sauce. In a medium saucepan, combine the remaining enchilada sauce with the beans. Cook over medium heat until thoroughly heated.

Soften the tortillas according to package directions. Place 1/8 of the turkey on each tortilla. Top each with 1/8 of the bean mixture. Sprinkle each with 1 tablespoon cheese. Roll up; place seam side down in the prepared baking dish. Top with the reserved enchilada sauce. Sprinkle with remaining cheese. Cover dish with the prepared foil. Bake for 15–20 minutes or until the cheese is melted.

Turkey Chili Casserole

2 tbsp. margarine, melted
2 tbsp. flour
2 c. milk
1 tbsp. Parmesan cheese
4 1/2 c. egg noodles, cooked
2 c. turkey, cooked, cubed
1 c. onions, chopped
1 1/2 c. bell pepper, chopped
1 tbsp. prepared mustard
2 tbsp. bread crumbs

Preheat oven to 375°F. Grease a 2-quart casserole dish and set aside. In a saucepan, melt margarine over medium-high heat; sprinkle with flour. Cook, whisking quickly and constantly, for 2 minutes.

Whisk in milk and parmesan cheese. Cook, stirring constantly, for another 2 minutes, until thickened. Remove from heat. Add noodles, turkey, onions, bell pepper, and mustard; toss to mix well.

Spoon mixture into prepared dish and sprinkle with bread crumbs. Bake for 20 minutes or until browned and bubbly.

Bean Sprouts and Turkey

2 c. turkey stock
1/3 c. whole wheat flour
1/2 c. carrots, chopped
1/2 c. onion, chopped
1/2 c. green pepper, chopped
1/2 c. celery, chopped
2 c. cooked turkey, diced
1 c. bean sprouts
2 c. brown rice, cooked

In a large saucepan, heat stock to boiling point. Transfer 1 1/4 cups of the stock to a 2-cup glass measuring cup. Stir flour into remaining stock.

Gradually add reserved hot stock, stirring constantly until thickened. Add all vegetables except sprouts and simmer for 20 minutes, or until vegetables are tender but not overcooked.

Add turkey and cook a few minutes longer. Add bean sprouts during the last two minutes. Serve over rice.

Dessert Recipes

Grease:
To apply a thin layer of butter, shortening, or oil to a pan or other equipment to prevent foods from sticking.

Knead:
To work dough into a uniform mixture by pressing, folding, stretching, and turning.

Zest:
To remove the outmost skin of citrus fruit with a knife, peeler, or zester.

World Class Pumpkin Pie

1 1/2 c. fresh pumpkin
1/2 c. brown sugar
1/2 c. granulated sugar
4 eggs
1 1/2 c. heavy cream
1/2 tsp. salt
1 tsp. cinnamon
1 tsp. nutmeg
1/2 tsp. ginger
1/2 tsp. cardamom
1/4 tsp. cloves
2 tsp. vanilla extract
2 tbsp. rum flavoring
1 pie crust shell, baked

Fill the bottom of a double boiler 1/3 full of water and bring to a boil.

In the top of the double boiler, combine all the ingredients, mixing well. Place over the boiling water. Stir with a wire whisk until the mixture is thick. Remove from heat. Pour the filling into the pre-baked pie crust. Allow to cool. Garnish as desired, and serve.

Pecan Candy Cake

1 1/3 c. candied red cherries, quartered
1 c. candied pineapple, coarsely chopped
1 1/2 c. pitted dates, coarsely chopped
1 tbsp. all-purpose flour
4 1/2 c. pecans, coarsely chopped
1 1/4 c. flaked coconut
1 can (14 oz.) sweetened condensed milk

Preheat oven to 250°F.
Grease and flour a 9 x 3-inch tube pan with a removable bottom; set aside. In a large bowl, combine the cherries, pineapple, and dates. Sprinkle with flour, tossing to coat.

Add pecans and coconut; toss to mix. Stir in the milk, mixing well. Spoon into the prepared pan, smoothing the top. Bake for 1 1/2 hours. Cool in the pan on a rack. Remove from the pan. Wrap the cake tightly in aluminum foil. Refrigerate for at least 2 weeks. Using a serrated knife, slice the cake into very thin pieces (cake is easier to cut when cold).

Pumpkin Ice Cream Pie

Crust:
1/3 c. butter, softened
2 c. cinnamon graham cracker crumbs

Filling:
1 qt. orange sherbet, slightly softened
1 can (16 oz.) pumpkin
1 pt. vanilla ice cream, slightly softened
1 tsp. vanilla extract
1 c. heavy cream, whipped stiff

Preheat oven to 375°F.

For the crust, mix the butter and cracker crumbs in a medium bowl until evenly moistened. Press along the bottom and sides of a 10-inch, deep-dish pie plate. Bake 8 minutes, or until lightly browned. Cool on a wire rack.

For the filling, place the orange sherbet in a large bowl. Fold in the pumpkin until just blended. Fold in the ice cream and vanilla extract until blended. Spoon into the crust, swirling the top. Freeze at least 4 hours, until hard. Up to 8 hours before serving, garnish with dollops of whipped cream. Return the pie to the freezer, removing about 10 minutes before serving.

Creamy Coconut Cake

Cake:
2 1/2 c. all-purpose flour
2 1/2 tsp. baking powder
1/2 tsp. salt
1 c. butter, softened
2 c. granulated sugar
4 eggs
1 c. milk
1 tsp. vanilla extract

Filling:
8 oz. whipping cream, beaten stiff
1/4 c. confectioners' sugar
1 tsp. vanilla extract
1/2 c. flaked coconut, divided
1/2 c. walnuts, chopped, divided

Frosting:
2 pkgs. (3 oz. each) cream cheese, softened
2 tbsp. butter, softened
4 c. confectioners' sugar
2 tsp. vanilla extract
milk (if needed)
1 pkg. (8 oz.) flaked coconut
1 c. walnuts, chopped

Preheat oven to 350°F. Grease and flour three 9-inch round pans.

To prepare the cake, combine the flour, baking powder, and salt; set aside.

Using an electric mixer set at high speed, mix the butter and 2 cups sugar until light. Add the eggs, one at a time, beating well after each addition. Continue beating, scraping the bowl occasionally with a rubber scraper, for 2 minutes, or until the mixture is light and fluffy. Turn the mixer to low speed and beat in the flour mixture in fourths, alternating with the milk in thirds, beginning and ending with the flour mixture.

Add the vanilla extract, beating just until smooth, about 1 minute. Pour into the prepared pans. Bake for 25–30 minutes, or until the surface springs back when lightly touched. Cool in the pans on wire racks for 10 minutes. Remove from pans and cool thoroughly.

For the filling, whip the cream, adding the sugar and vanilla extract. Refrigerate until the cake has completely cooled.

To prepare the frosting, cream together the cream cheese and butter. Add the sugar and vanilla extract. Stir in a little milk, if needed to achieve the desired consistency.

After the cake layers have completely cooled, place the first layer on a serving plate. Spread the top with half of the whipped cream filling. Sprinkle with 1/4 cup coconut and 1/4 cup chopped walnuts.

Place the second layer on top and spread with the remaining filling. Sprinkle with 1/4 cup coconut and 1/4 cup walnuts. Place the final layer on top.

Frost the top and sides of the cake (use skewers to hold the cake in place while frosting, if necessary). Cover the entire cake with coconut and sprinkle with chopped walnuts. Refrigerate to set the frosting.

Yule Log

Cake:
5 eggs
3/4 c. cake flour
3/4 tsp. baking powder
1/4 tsp. salt
3/4 c. sugar, divided
1 tsp. vanilla extract

Filling:
1/2 c. confectioners' sugar
1 egg yolk
1 pinch salt
1 1/2 tsp. vanilla extract
6 tbsp. heavy cream, divided
1/2 c. butter, softened
30 whole chestnuts, cooked
2 1/3 c. confectioners' sugar, divided
2 tbsp. butter

Mocha Frosting:
2 tsp. instant coffee
1 1/4 c. confectioners' sugar
3 tbsp. cocoa
5 1/3 tbsp. butter
1 1/2 tbsp. corn syrup
1 tsp. vanilla extract
2 tbsp. heavy cream

Garnish:
cherry halves
angelica
cranberries
holly

Preheat oven to 400°F. Grease a 10 x 15 x 1-inch jelly roll pan. Line the bottom and sides with waxed paper, and grease the paper.

For the cake, bring the eggs to room temperature and separate.

Mix the flour, baking powder, and salt; set aside.

Beat the egg yolks until thick and pale. Gradually add 6 tablespoons sugar, beating well after each addition. The mixture should fall in a thick ribbon when the beaters are lifted. Add the vanilla extract and beat again.

Using clean, dry beaters, beat the egg whites until foamy. Gradually add the remaining sugar, beating constantly, until the whites stand in firm, glossy, moist peaks. Fold one-third of the whites into the yolk mixture; then fold in the remaining whites. Gradually fold the flour mixture into the egg mixture, folding gently but thoroughly. Spread the batter evenly in the prepared pan.

Immediately place the pan in the oven. Bake for 10–12 minutes, or until the cake is golden on top and a tester comes out clean. Do not over bake.

Remove the cake from the oven. Working quickly, first cover the pan with a clean towel, then with an inverted cookie sheet. Turn the pan over, using the towel and sheet to turn out the cake. Remove the pan and peel off the waxed paper. Slide the towel and cake on to a counter. The cake is wrong side up at this point.

Cut off any crisp edges. Fold one end of the towel over the short end of the cake and roll the cake in the towel. (At this point, the towel should actually be rolled up inside the cake roll.) Place the rolled cake, seam side down, on a wire rack to cool completely.

To prepare the buttercream filling, combine 1/2 cup confectioners' sugar, egg yolk, salt, vanilla extract, and 3 tablespoons cream. Beat for 8 minutes at medium speed. Without washing the beaters, cream 1/2 cup butter until it is light. Add the yolk mixture a little at a time, beating well after each addition. Gradually add 1 cup confectioners' sugar, beating well after each addition. Set aside.

Purée the chestnuts with 2 tablespoons butter, 3 tablespoons cream, and 1 1/3 cups confectioners' sugar. Stir the chestnut purée into the buttercream, blending thoroughly. Thin with a little more cream, if necessary, to bring it to an easily spreadable consistency.

For the frosting, powder the instant coffee by placing it in a plastic bag and crushing with a rolling pin. Mix together the powdered coffee, confectioners' sugar, and cocoa. Add the remaining ingredients and beat for 1 minute at medium speed. Add a little more cream, if necessary, to bring it to an easily spreadable consistency.

Unroll the cooled cake, leaving it on the towel. Spread 1/2 cup frosting evenly over the cake to the edges. Spread 2 cups of filling over the frosting, pushing a generous amount into the curved end of the cake. Re-roll the cake, without the towel but using it to help roll. Place the cake, seam side down, on a cake plate or tray. Remove any excess filling from the ends and seam edge. Refrigerate for 1 hour to set the filling.

Trim a thin slice from one end of the chilled cake. Cut and reserve a wedge from other end. Spread a small amount of filling on the top center of the cake and press the reserved wedge on it to make the "knothole." Frost entire cake with the remaining frosting, building the frosting up around the sides of the knothole. Be sure not to cover the top of the knothole. Work the frosting as far under the roll as possible. Repeatedly draw a narrow metal spatula through the frosting to simulate the bark texture.

Garnish with cherry halves and pieces of angelica cut into leaf shapes. Refrigerate until ready to serve. Just before serving, surround cake with holly and cranberries.

Christmas Eggnog Pound Cake

1 c. butter, softened
1 c. shortening
3 c. sugar
6 eggs
3 c. all-purpose flour
1 c. dairy eggnog
1 c. flaked coconut
1 tsp. lemon extract
1 tsp. vanilla extract
1 tsp. coconut extract

Preheat oven to 325°F.

Cream together the butter and shortening. Gradually add the sugar, beating well. Add the eggs, one at a time, beating well after each addition. Alternately add the flour and eggnog to the creamed mixture, beginning and ending with the flour. Stir in the coconut and extracts; blend well. Pour the batter into a greased and floured 10-inch tube pan. Bake for 1 1/2 hours. Cool in the pan for 10 minutes before turning out on a serving platter.

Cranberry Upside Down Cake

6 oz. butter, softened, divided
3/4 c. light brown sugar
24 oz. fresh cranberries
1 c. granulated sugar
2 egg yolks
1 tsp. vanilla extract
1 1/2 c. all-purpose flour
2 tsp. baking powder
1/4 tsp. salt
1/2 c. milk
2 egg whites

Preheat oven to 350°F.

In a 9-inch round cake pan, melt 2 ounces of butter with the brown sugar over low heat, stirring constantly until sugar is completely dissolved. Pour cranberries over brown sugar and butter mixture. Set aside.

Cream the remaining butter with the granulated sugar until smooth. Stir in the egg yolks and vanilla extract. In a large bowl, combine flour, baking powder, and salt. Alternately add flour mixture and milk to the egg yolk mixture. Stir only until mixed. Beat the egg whites until stiff peaks form. Fold them into the cake mixture. Pour cake mixture over the cranberries. Bake for 50–60 minutes.

Amaretto Apples

2 Golden Delicious apples
1 1/2 tbsp. unsalted butter
2 tbsp. sugar
2 tbsp. raisins
2 tbsp. amaretto liqueur
2 tbsp. almonds, sliced, toasted
whipped cream

Peel apples, core, cut into 1/2-inch dice and set aside. Melt butter in medium skillet over medium-high heat. Add apples; sprinkle with sugar and sauté until tender, about 6 minutes. Stir in raisins. Add liqueur and cook until liquid reduces to glaze, about 1 minute. Divide between 2 dessert dishes. Garnish with almonds and whipped cream. Serve immediately.

Apple Raisin Crisp

1/2 c. raisins
1/2 c. rolled oats
1/2 c. brown sugar
1/4 c. all-purpose flour
1/2 tsp. cinnamon
1/4 c. butter
1/2 c. pecans, chopped
6 apples, peeled, cored, sliced
2 tbsp. sugar

In a small mixing bowl, pour enough boiling water over the raisins to cover them. Let stand for 5 minutes, then drain raisins.

For topping, in a medium mixing bowl, stir together rolled oats, brown sugar, flour, and cinnamon. Using a pastry blender, cut in butter until mixture resembles coarse crumbs. Stir in chopped pecans. Set topping aside.

For filling, in large mixing bowl, combine drained raisins, sliced apples, and sugar. Gently toss until combined. Transfer the filling to an ungreased 9 X 9 X 2-inch baking pan. Sprinkle topping on the filling. Bake in a 375°F oven for 30-35 minutes or until the apples are tender and topping is golden. Serve warm.

Caramel Apple Bread Pudding

28 caramels
1/4 c. water
4 c. bread cubes
4 c. apples, peeled, sliced
5 eggs, slightly beaten
2 c. milk
1/4 c. sugar
1 tsp. vanilla
1/4 tsp. salt
1/4 tsp. cinnamon

Melt caramels with water in a covered double boiler or in a saucepan over low heat. Stir occasionally until sauce is smooth. Place bread cubes in greased 12 x 8-inch baking dish. Top with apple slices. Combine eggs, milk, sugar, vanilla, salt, and cinnamon; pour over apples. Cover with caramel sauce. Set dish in large pan on oven rack; pour in boiling water to 1/2-inch depth. Bake at 325°F for 1 hour and 20 minutes or until knife inserted halfway between center and outside edge comes out clean. Serve hot or cold.

Devil's Food With Fudge Frosting

Cake:
1 3/4 c. cake flour, sifted
1/2 c. cocoa
1 tsp. baking soda
1/2 tsp. salt
1/2 c. unsalted butter
1 1/4 c. granulated sugar
1 1/2 tsp. vanilla
2 eggs
1 c. boiling water

Frosting:
1/4 c. unsalted butter
2 c. confectioners' sugar
2 oz. unsweetened chocolate, melted
1 1/2 tsp. vanilla extract
2 tbsp. evaporated milk

Preheat oven to 350°F. Grease 2 8-inch cake pans, then dust generously with cocoa. Set aside. Sift the flour, cocoa, baking soda, and salt onto a piece of waxed paper and set it aside. Cream the butter until fluffy, add the sugar and vanilla, and continue beating until the batter is silvery and light.

Beat the eggs in one by one, then add the sifted dry ingredients alternately with the boiling water, beginning and ending with the dry ingredients. Beat well after each addition.

Divide the batter equally between the two pans, smoothing the tops. Bake the layers uncovered for 30–35 minutes, or until the layers feel spongy to the touch and begin to pull away from the sides of the pans. Cool the layers upright in pans on wire racks for 10 minutes, then carefully loosen around the edges with a spatula and turn onto wire racks. Cool completely before frosting.

Frosting:
Cream the butter until it is light, then add the confectioners' sugar gradually, beating all the while. Beat in the melted chocolate and vanilla, then add just enough cream to make the frosting a good consistency for spreading.

Sandwich the two cake layers together with frosting, then frost the top and sides of the cake. Swirl the frosting into peaks and valleys.

Easy Fig Pie

14 fig cookies
2 c. milk
1 pkg. vanilla pudding mix
1/2 c. light molasses
1 tsp. cinnamon
1/2 tsp. allspice
1 tsp. vanilla
1/2 tsp. salt
1 10-inch pie shell, cooled
Whipped cream

Crumble fig cookies into milk. Add pudding mix. Stir over heat until pudding bubbles. Remove from heat and stir in molasses, cinnamon, and allspice. Add vanilla and salt. Cool. Place in cooled pie shell. Top with whipped cream.

Festive Raisin Tarts

1 pkg. (11 oz.) pastry mix
1 c. raisins
1/2 c. walnuts
1/2 c. brown sugar, packed
3 tbsp. butter, softened
3 tbsp. orange juice
1 egg, beaten
2 1/2 tbsp. half-and-half
whipped cream

Prepare pastry according to package directions. Line small tart pans with pastry. Place on baking sheet. Finely chop raisins and walnuts; combine with brown sugar, butter, orange juice, egg and half-and-half. Bake on lower rack at 425°F about 20 minutes, or until pastry is lightly browned. Top with whipped cream.

Grasshopper Pie

Crust:
1 1/2 c. chocolate wafer crumbs, fine
1/4 c. sugar
1/4 c. unsalted butter

Filling:
1 1/2 tsp. unflavored gelatin
1 1/3 c. heavy cream, well chilled
1/4 c. sugar
1/4 c. green creme de menthe
1/4 c. white creme de cacao
4 egg yolks

Garnish:
Mint flavored chocolate, grated

In a bowl, cream together the wafer crumbs, sugar, and butter until combined. Pat mixture onto bottom and sides of a buttered 9-inch pie plate. Bake in the middle of a preheated 450°F oven for 5 minutes. Allow to cool completely.

In a metal bowl, sprinkle the gelatin over 1/3 cup of the cream and let it soften for 5 minutes. Whisk in the sugar, creme de menthe, creme de cacao, and the egg yolks. Set the bowl over a saucepan of simmering water, whisking constantly, until it measures 160°F on a candy thermometer. Transfer the custard to an ice water bath and stir until it is cooled and thickened. In another bowl, beat the remaining cream until it holds stiff peaks. Fold it into the custard.

Pour the filling into the crust and chill the pie for at least 4 hours or until it is set. Sprinkle with grated chocolate and serve.

Candies & Cookies

Sift:
To put dry ingredients, such as flour, through a sifter or sieve.

Stir:
To mix ingredients with a spoon using a circular motion.

Whip:
To beat rapidly to increase the volume of an ingredient such as cream or egg whites.

Holiday Butter Creme Mints

4 tbsp. butter, softened
3 tbsp. sweetened condensed milk
4 c. confectioners' sugar
1/2 tsp. spearmint flavoring
2 drops green food coloring
2 drops red food coloring
granulated sugar

Blend softened butter and condensed milk together. Gradually add the confectioners' sugar until mixture becomes stiff. Add flavoring in small amounts until desired flavor is reached.

Separate the mixture into two evenly divided bowls. Add green food coloring to one bowl, a little at a time, until the desired color is reached. Repeat the process with the other bowl using the red food coloring.

Roll the mixtures into small balls. Roll the balls in granulated sugar. Press each ball into a candy mold and unmold at once. Store in an airtight container.

Makes 90 candies.

Heavenly Coconut Cookies

3 1/2 c. flaked coconut, divided
2 c. flour
1 c. butter
1/4 tsp. salt
1 c. sugar
1/2 tsp. baking soda
1 tsp. vanilla extract
1 egg
1 egg yolk
1 tbsp. cream
4 dozen pecan halves

Combine 2 cups flaked coconut, flour, butter, salt, sugar, baking soda, vanilla extract, and egg; mix well. Shape into logs. Roll each log in the remaining coconut to coat. Freeze the logs.

When ready to bake, preheat oven to 350°F.

Mix together the egg yolk and cream. Cut the frozen logs into 1/4-inch thick slices. Brush each with the egg yolk mixture. Press a pecan half into each cookie. Bake 15 minutes, or until the edges are golden brown.

Sugar Cookies

2 eggs
2/3 c. vegetable oil
2 tsp. vanilla extract
1 tsp. lemon peel, grated
3/4 c. sugar
2 c. flour
2 tsp. baking powder
1/2 tsp. salt

Preheat oven to 350°F.

Beat the eggs with a fork until well blended. Stir in the oil, vanilla extract, and lemon peel. Blend in the sugar until the mixture thickens; set aside.

Sift together the flour, baking powder, and salt. Stir into the egg mixture. Drop by teaspoonfuls 2 inches apart on an ungreased cookie sheet. Stamp each cookie flat with the bottom of a lightly oiled glass dipped in sugar.

Bake for 8–10 minutes. Immediately remove cookies from the cookie sheet.

Homemade Caramel Corn

2 bags air-popped popcorn, popped
1 box brown sugar
1 c. butter
1/2 c. light Karo syrup
1 tsp. vanilla extract
1/2 tsp. baking soda

Preheat oven to 250°F.

Grease an aluminum roaster pan. Pop enough popcorn to fill it. Place the popcorn in the prepared pan.

Combine the brown sugar, butter, and syrup in a saucepan. Melt and bring to a boil. Remove from heat and add the vanilla extract and baking soda. Stir until well blended. Pour over the popcorn and mix until coated. Bake for 1 hour, turning occasionally.

Gingerbread

1 c. granulated sugar
1/4 tsp. salt
1 tsp. ginger
1/2 tsp. cinnamon
1/2 tsp. confectioners' sugar
1/2 tsp. cloves
1 c. vegetable oil
1 c. light molasses
2 tsp. baking soda
1 c. boiling water
2 1/2 c. all-purpose flour, unsifted
2 eggs, well beaten

Preheat oven to 350°F.

In a bowl, mix the granulated sugar, salt, ginger, cinnamon, confectioners' sugar, and cloves. Add the vegetable oil and molasses, stirring until well blended.

Mix the baking soda in the boiling water and immediately stir the mixture into the batter. Gradually add the flour, mixing well after each addition. Mix in the beaten eggs. Pour into a greased 9 x 13-inch baking pan. Bake for 40 minutes. Serve with a garnish of whipped cream, if desired.

Pumpkin Bars

1 pkg. spice cake mix (2-layer size), divided
1/2 c. butter, melted
3 eggs
1 c. canned pumpkin
1/2 c. sugar
1/2 tsp. orange peel, grated
1/2 c. pecans, chopped
1/8 tsp. salt

Preheat oven to 350°F.

Reserve 2/3 cup of the cake mix.

In a large bowl, combine the remaining cake mix, butter, and 1 egg; mix well. Pat into a well-greased, 13 x 9 x 2-inch baking pan. Bake for 15 minutes.

Combine the reserved cake mix, pumpkin, sugar, 2 eggs, grated orange peel, and salt. Using an electric mixer, beat at medium speed for 1–2 minutes. Pour over partially baked layer. Top with nuts. Bake 15–20 minutes, or until set. Cool and cut into bars. Store in the refrigerator.

Hard Candy

2 c. sugar
2/3 c. light Karo syrup
3/4 c. water
1 tsp. oil flavor
food coloring
1 tsp. citric acid
confectioners' sugar

Spray the inside and surfaces of candy molds with non-stick cooking spray; set aside.

Stir together all ingredients except the confectioners' sugar. Pour into a saucepan (use a thin pan to avoid over cooking). Bring the mixture to a boil.

Cover for 3 minutes. Add a candy thermometer, but do not stir. When the temperature reaches 285–290°F, remove from heat.

Allow the temperature to cool to 255°F, then add the flavor, color, and citric acid. Be sure to cover the pan after adding the citric acid so that the taste won't fade.

Pour the cooked candy into the prepared molds, using a candy funnel sprayed with non-stick cooking spray.

Dust the finished candies with confectioners' sugar to keep them from sticking together.

Divinity

1/2 c. light corn syrup
2 1/2 c. sugar
1/4 tsp. salt
1/2 c. water
2 egg whites
1 tsp. vanilla extract
1 c. nuts, coarsely chopped

In a saucepan, mix the syrup, sugar, salt, and water. Cook, stirring constantly, until the sugar is dissolved.

Continue to cook, without stirring, until the temperature reaches 248°F on a candy thermometer, or until the mixture forms a firm ball when a small amount of it is dropped in cold water.

Beat the egg whites until they are stiff, but not dry. Slowly pour about half of the syrup mixture over the egg whites, beating constantly.

Cook the remaining syrup until the temperature reaches 272°F, or until hard threads form when a small amount is dropped in cold water. Slowly add the syrup to the egg white mixture, beating until the mixture holds its shape. Stir in the vanilla extract and nuts. Drop by spoonfuls on waxed paper.

Variations:

Holiday Divinity:
Stir in 1/4 cup chopped candied cherries and 1/4 cup chopped candied pineapple along with the nuts.

Chocolate Divinity:
Add 6 ounces semi-sweet chocolate chips along with the vanilla extract. Beat until well blended.

Peanut Butter Brittle

2 c. sugar
1/2 c. light corn syrup
1/2 c. water
1/3 c. chunky peanut butter
1 tsp. baking soda

Grease 2 large baking sheets and place them on wire racks.

In a heavy 1 1/2-quart saucepan, combine the sugar, syrup, and water. Bring to a boil over medium heat, stirring constantly. Cook, continuing to stir, until the mixture reaches 300°F on a candy thermometer. Stir in the peanut butter, blending well. Remove from heat.

Quickly, but gently, stir in the soda. Immediately pour the mixture on the cookie sheets. Do not spread. Let stand for 3–5 minutes until mixture is cool enough to handle. When slightly cooled, grasp candy by the edges, lifting slightly, and pull it as thin as possible. Allow to cool completely. Break into pieces. Store in an airtight container.

Peanut Butter Buckeyes

1 c. butter
16 oz. confectioners' sugar
12 oz. crunchy peanut butter
12 oz. semi-sweet chocolate chips
4 oz. paraffin

Combine butter, sugar, and peanut butter in a medium bowl. Blend until smooth. Roll into 1-inch balls. Chill.

Place the chocolate chips and paraffin in the top of a double boiler and melt over hot, but not boiling, water. Drop the peanut butter balls, one at a time, into mixture to coat. Place on waxed paper to cool.

Christmas Candy Cane Cookies

2 1/2 c. flour
1 tsp. salt
1 c. confectioners' sugar
1 c. shortening, softened
1 egg
1 tsp. vanilla extract
1 1/2 tsp. almond extract
red or green food coloring
1 tsp. peppermint extract

Preheat oven to 375°F.

In a large bowl, combine all ingredients except the food coloring and peppermint; mix well.

Divide the dough into 2 equal parts, placing each half in a separate bowl. Add red (or green) food coloring to one of the bowls, mixing well until desired color is achieved. Add peppermint extract to the colored dough.

Break off pieces of each color of dough. Roll each piece into a 4-inch long strip. Twist the two colors of strips together. Place the twist on a cookie sheet. Shape the top of each twist into a hook, so that it resembles a candy cane. Bake for 15 minutes.

White Fudge

1 1/3 c. sugar
1/2 c. butter
2/3 c. cream
1/8 tsp. salt
1/2 lb. white chocolate, finely chopped
2 c. miniature marshmallows
1/2 tsp. vanilla extract

Cook first 4 ingredients without stirring to 238°F. Remove from heat and add the next 3 ingredients. Blend well. Pack into a 9-inch square pan. When partially cool, cut into squares. Other colors of chocolate (pink, green, yellow, butterscotch) can be added instead of white.

Apricot Coconut Balls

1 1/2 c. dried apricots, finely chopped
2 c. coconut, shredded
2/3 c. sweetened condensed milk
Powdered sugar

Mix apricots and coconut. Add condensed milk and blend well. Shape into balls and roll in powdered sugar. Let stand until firm.

Crystal Almonds

1 1/4 c. brown sugar
1/4 c. heavy cream
1 tbsp. butter
1/2 tsp. cinnamon
1/8 tsp. salt
1 tsp. vanilla extract
2 1/2 c. whole almonds

Combine sugar, cream, butter, cinnamon and salt in a 2-quart saucepan. Mix and bring to boil over medium heat. Cook to 244°F (firm ball stage), stirring constantly. Remove from heat, then add vanilla and nuts. Continue stirring until candy grains on nuts. Spread on cookie sheet and allow to cool before breaking apart.

Holiday Truffles

6 oz. semi-sweet chocolate chips
1 can sweetened condensed milk
2 tbsp. almond flavored liqueur
1/4 tsp. almond extract
2 tbsp. orange liqueur

In heavy pan, over low heat, melt chips with sweetened condensed milk. Remove from heat; divide into 2 bowls. To one bowl, add almond liqueur and almond extract. To the other bowl, add orange flavored liqueur. Chill 1 hour. Shape into one-inch balls. Roll in coatings if desired. Chill until firm (1 hour). Store covered at room temperature.

Heavenly Hash

4 tbsp. unsweetened chocolate, grated
2 c. sugar
1 c. cream
1 tbsp. butter
2 tbsp. marshmallow cream
1/2 c. pecans, chopped
1/2 c. almonds, blanched and roasted
1 tsp. vanilla extract
24 marshmallows

Combine chocolate and sugar. Add cream and butter. Boil to soft ball stage (234°F - 238°F). Remove from heat. Add marshmallow cream, nuts, and flavoring. Beat until mixture begins to thicken. Place marshmallows on well buttered dish. Pour mixture over them. Let cool; cut in squares.

Coconut Bon Bons

15 oz. sweetened condensed milk
1/2 c. butter
2 c. confectioners' sugar
12 oz. coconut, grated, dried
24 oz. semi-sweet chocolate
4 tbsp. shortening

Mix together condensed milk, butter, sugar and coconut. Cover with waxed paper and chill for 24 hours. Melt chocolate with shortening. Roll coconut mixture into balls and with fork, dip into chocolate. Drop on waxed paper to cool and dry.

Peppermint Fudge Squares

2/3 c. evaporated milk
1 2/3 c. sugar
2 tbsp. butter
1/2 tsp. salt
2 c. miniature marshmallows
1 1/2 c. chocolate chips
1/2 tsp. peppermint extract
1/2 c. walnuts, chopped

Mix milk, sugar, butter and salt in a pot. Bring to a full boil, then boil for 5 minutes stirring constantly. Remove from heat.

Add marshmallows, chocolate chips, peppermint and walnuts. Stir vigorously until marshmallows are melted and thoroughly blended.

Pour into 8-inch square pan. Chill.

Makes about 2 pounds.

Layered Mint Chocolate Candy

10 squares semi-sweet chocolate
1 large can sweetened condensed milk, divided
2 tsp. vanilla
1 pkg. white chocolate squares
1 tbsp. peppermint extract
6 drops green food coloring

In heavy saucepan, over low heat, melt semi-sweet chocolate with 1 cup sweetened condensed milk. Remove from heat; stir in vanilla.

Spread half the mixture onto waxed paper lined 8-inch square pan. Chill 10 minutes, or until firm.

Hold remaining chocolate mixture at room temperature.

In heavy saucepan, over low heat, melt white chocolate with remaining sweetened condensed milk. Remove from heat; stir in peppermint extract and food coloring. Spread on chilled chocolate layer. Chill 10 minutes longer, or until firm.

Spread reserved melted chocolate mixture on mint layer. Chill 2 hours, or until firm. Turn onto cutting board. Peel off paper and cut into squares.

Store loosely covered at room temperature.

Index

Hors d'oeuvres & Beverages 5
A Bloomin' Onion 10
Apple-Stuffed Mushrooms 9
Bacon-Wrapped Scallops 9
Barbecued Chicken Wings 6
Cheese Fondue 11
Cheese Log 11
Chicken Liver Spread 11
Chicken Squares 7
Chili con Queso 7
Christmas Avocado Balls 10
Christmas Punch 9
Crackin' Jack 12
Holiday Eggnog 9
Holiday Pine Cones 10
Hot Crab Bites 12
Orange Wassail 7
Potstickers 8
Roasted Garlic &
   Broccoli Cheese Spread 7
Shrimp Dip 6
Spicy Cheese Ball 12
Spicy Crab Dip 6
Spinach Dip 6

Entrées 13
Apple Cider Turkey 18
Apple Juice Roast 16
Apple Pork Tenderloin 16
Autumn Fruited Chicken 19
Baked Cornish Hens 20
Baked Pineapple Chicken 20
Basil-Stuffed Lamb Roast 17
Braised Breast of
   Duck with Peaches 20
Champagne Chicken 21
Chicken & Dumplings 21
Chicken and Sweet Potatoes 22
Grilled Turkey 15
Holiday Beef Rib Eye Roast 14
Holiday Baked Oysters 22
Holiday Turkey Fillets 19
Leg of Lamb with Apricot
   Mustard Glaze 17
Pear and Maple Pork Chops 15
Pork Chops with Stuffing 15
Roast Duck with Orange Sauce 14
Salmon in Red Wine with Apricots 18
Seasoned Ham 14

Stuffings & Gravies 23
Apple and Bacon
   Cornbread Stuffing 27
Almond Sausage Stuffing 24
Basting Sauce for Roast 28
Béarnaise Sauce 28
Blender Gravy 28
Brown Sauce 24
Madeira Gravy 26
Mint Sauce 28
Sage Dressing 26
Sausage and Wild Rice Stuffing 26
Sweet and Sour Sauce 26
Turkey Giblet Gravy 27
Turkey Gravy 25
Turkey with Oyster Stuffing 25
Wild Rice Stuffing 24

Vegetables & Side Dishes 29
Acorn Squash
   with Cranberry Stuffing 30
Baked Carrots 34
Braised Red Cabbage
   with Currants 34
Broiled Eggplant
   with Walnut Sauce 35
Brussels Sprouts
   in Mustard Sauce 35
Butter Pecan Squash 35
Cauliflower au Gratin 30
Cheesy Garlic Potatoes 31
Corn Vegetable Medley 30
Cranberry Fruit Salad 31
Crispy String Beans 31
Elegant Stuffed Pumpkin 32
Glazed Pearl Onions 32
Grapefruit Sweet Potatoes 36
Holiday Coleslaw 30
Homestyle Spinach 33
Maple-Glazed Carrots 33
Parmesan Asparagus Spears 33
Pecan Chicken and Rice 36
Red and Green Potato Salad 34
Roasted Sweet Corn 34
Sweet Garden Peas with Mint 31
Vegetable Hash 36
Winter Squash with Cranberries 32

Casseroles 37
Apple-Squash Casserole 38
Artichoke Spinach Casserole 38
Baked Green Tomato Casserole 38
Broccoli Casserole 38
Cabbage Roll Casserole 39
Chicken and Dumpling Casserole 42
Christmas Ham and
   Noodle Casserole 41
Christmas Potato Casserole 39
Crabmeat Casserole 41
Golden Crumb Broccoli 42
Green Bean and Onion Casserole 41
Ham, Apples, and
   Sweet Potato Casserole 40
Onion Mushroom Casserole 40
Papa John's Sweet Potato Casserole
   with Pecan Topping 39
Tater Tot Casserole 42
Yellow Squash Casserole 40
Zucchini Stuffing Casserole 40

Leftover Solutions 43
Baked Turkey and Ham Hash 47
Bean Sprouts and Turkey 48
Swiss Broccoli Pie 45
Turkey Broccoli Bake 44
Turkey Broccoli Mushroom Bake 45
Turkey Chili Casserole 48
Turkey Enchiladas 48
Turkey Meatloaf 44
Turkey Pie with Biscuit Crust 46
Turkey Strata 47
White Bean Turkey Chili 47
Wild Mushroom and Turkey Pasta 44

Dessert Recipes 49
Amaretto Apples 54
Apple Raisin Crisp 54
Caramel Apple Bread Pudding 55
Christmas Eggnog Pound Cake 53
Cranberry Upside Down Cake 54
Creamy Coconut Cake 51
Devil's Food with Fudge Frosting 55
Easy Fig Pie 56
Festive Raisin Tarts 56
Grasshopper Pie 56
Pecan Candy Cake 50
Pumpkin Ice Cream Pie 50
World Class Pumpkin Pie 50
Yule Log 52

Candies & Cookies 57
Apricot Coconut Balls 62
Christmas Candy Cane Cookies 61
Coconut Bon Bons 63
Crystal Almonds 62
Divinity 60
Gingerbread 59
Hard Candy 60
Heavenly Coconut Cookies 58
Heavenly Hash 62
Holiday Butter Creme Mints 58
Holiday Truffles 62
Homemade Caramel Corn 59
Layered Mint Chocolate Candy 63
Peanut Butter Brittle 61
Peanut Butter Buckeyes 61
Peppermint Fudge Squares 63
Pumpkin Bars 59
Sugar Cookies 58
White Fudge 62